Teacher's Pack INTRO

CONTEMPORARY TOPICS

Academic Listening and Note-Taking Skills

Jeanette Clement
Cynthia Lennox

Michael Rost
SERIES EDITOR

PEARSON
Longman

Contemporary Topics Introductory: High Beginner
Academic Listening and Note-Taking Skills

Pearson Education, 10 Bank Street, White Plains, NY 10606

Staff credits: The people who made up the *Contemporary Topics Introductory* team, representing editorial, production, design, and manufacturing, are Rhea Banker, Danielle Belfiore, Dave Dickey, Christine Edmonds, Nancy Flaggman, Dana Klinek, Amy McCormick, Linda Moser, Carlos Rountree, Jennifer Stem, Leigh Stolle, Paula Van Ells, Kenneth Volcjak, and Pat Wosczyk.
Cover design: Ann France
Text composition: ElectraGraphics, Inc.
Text font: 11/13 Times
Credits: See page 62

ISBN-10: 0-13-207520-2
ISBN-13: 978-0-13-207520-6

PEARSON LONGMAN ON THE WEB

Pearsonlongman.com offers online resources for teachers and students. Access our Companion Websites, our online catalog, and our local offices around the world.

Visit us at **www.pearsonlongman.com**.

Printed in the United States of America
2 3 4 5 6 7 8 9 10—OPM—14 13 12 11 10 09

CONTENTS

INTRODUCTION

The *Contemporary Topics* series provides a stimulating, content-based approach that helps students develop their listening, note-taking, and discussion skills while studying relevant topics. Each unit centers around a short academic lecture, with topics drawn from a range of disciplines.

The lectures feature engaging instructors with live student audiences, and take place in authentic lecture hall settings. The multimodal design of each lecture allows for various learning formats for DVD users, including audio- or video-only presentations, optional subtitling, Presentation Points slide support, and pop-up Coaching Tips.

In order to maximize the benefits of content-based instruction, the *Contemporary Topics* series has developed a carefully sequenced eight-step learning methodology. This introduction provides an overview of each of these steps.

Step 1: Connect to the Topic *Estimated Time: 10 minutes* This opening section
invites students to activate what they already know about the unit topic by connecting it to their own experiences and beliefs. Typically, students fill out a short survey and compare answers with a partner. The teacher acts as a facilitator, having students share ideas about the topic before they explore it further.

Basic Procedure:

- Set the tone for the unit by talking about the image(s) on the page or related current news events.
- Read the introductory paragraph aloud, paraphrasing as necessary.
- Have students complete the survey/activity.
- Ask students to compare answers with a partner, or discuss answers casually as a class.

Methodology Focus: The actual content of students' responses in this initial activity is not as important as their attempt to understand and interact. It is important that all students participate in activating their ideas about the theme of the unit. This engagement helps set the tone of "active listening" throughout the unit. Having students compare answers with a partner helps ensure that every student is on task and thinking about the unit topic.

Step 2: Build Your Vocabulary *Estimated Time: 15 minutes* This section
familiarizes students with the key content words and phrases from the lecture. Each lecture contains 10–15 key words from the Academic Word List to ensure that students learn core vocabulary needed for academic success. Students read and *listen to* target words in context so that they can better prepare for the upcoming lecture. Students then complete exercises to get an initial understanding of the target lexis of the unit. Interact with Vocabulary! is a supplementary activity that focuses on the syntax and collocations of new vocabulary in the unit.

Basic Procedure:

- Have students listen to the sentences or paragraphs.

- Have students guess the meaning of each boldfaced word and choose the best definition.

- If time permits, try the Interact with Vocabulary! activity to enable students to focus on form as they learn new words and collocations.

Methodology Focus: Vocabulary knowledge and the ability to recognize vocabulary as it is spoken are key predictors of listening comprehension. As such, spending some pre-listening time on recognizing key vocabulary from the lecture will usually increase students' comprehension of the ideas in the lecture. It's best to spend 10–15 minutes on vocabulary preparation. More than this may give students the impression that vocabulary learning is overly important. Research shows that multiple exposures to new words in context is necessary for vocabulary acquisition, so it's not essential that students "master" the vocabulary in this section. Frequent reviews of the vocabulary sections will aid in acquisition.

Step 3: Focus Your Attention   *Estimated Time: 10 minutes* In this section, students learn strategies for listening actively and taking clear notes. Because a major part of "active listening" involves a readiness to deal with comprehension difficulties, this section provides specific tips to help students direct their attention and gain more control of how they listen. The Try It Out! section, based on a short audio extract, allows students to work on listening and note-taking strategies before they get to the main lecture. Typically, examples of actual notes are provided to give students concrete "starter models."

Basic Procedure:

- Go through this section carefully, reading explanations aloud. Draw attention to examples.

- Play the audio for Try It Out! in order to have students experience the given technique.

- After you play the audio extract once or twice, have students compare answers and/or notes with a partner.

Methodology Focus: Active listening involves a number of component strategies for focusing students' attention: predicting, guessing (i.e. using available knowledge to make good guesses), filling in gaps and making connections, monitoring areas where they don't understand, asking questions, and responding personally. Above all, active listening involves curiosity and a desire to understand more deeply. This section provides tips for focusing students' attention that, when learned incrementally, will help them become more active listeners. It is important that students find a specific way to control their attention and concentration as they listen.

Step 4: Listen to the Lecture   *Estimated Time: 20–30 minutes* As the central section of each unit, Listen to the Lecture allows for two full listening cycles: one to focus on "top-down listening" strategies (Listen for Main Ideas) and one to focus on "bottom-up listening" strategies (Listen for Details). In keeping with the principles of content-based instruction, students are provided with several layers of support. In the Before You Listen section, students are guided to activate concepts and vocabulary they already know or studied earlier in the unit.

The lecture can be viewed in video mode or just listened to in audio mode. In video mode, the lecture can be accompanied by the speaker's Presentation Points or by subtitles for reinforcing comprehension (recommended as a final review). Coaching Tips on strategies for listening, note-taking, and critical thinking can also be turned on.

Basic Procedure:

Before You Listen

- Have students go through this section explicitly—for instance, actually writing down a "prediction" when asked.

Listen for Main Ideas

- Have students *close their books* and take notes as they listen.
- Play the lecture through or pause at times. If pausing, it's best to do so at episode boundaries (see Audioscripts in this Teacher's Pack), as these are natural pausing points.
- Have students complete the exercise, working alone, using their notes.
- Check answers, or play the lecture again so students can confirm their answers. If repeating the lecture, have students confirm and expand their notes with books closed.

Listen for Details

- Play the lecture one more time, again with students confirming and expanding their notes. Then have students complete the Listen for Details exercise.

Methodology Focus: The lecture itself is the focal point of each unit, and therefore the focal point of the content-based approach. In this approach, students of course learn grammar, vocabulary, and pronunciation, but always within the context of relevant content, which may make it more memorable. We recommend that you focus on helping students understand the content of each lecture as deeply as possible, and work on specific language skills during the Talk about the Topic, Review Your Notes, and Extend the Topic sections. To better understand the lecture, students can work on two kinds of exercises: "Top-down listening" generally refers to "getting the gist" of what is said, not focusing on all of the details. "Bottom-up listening" generally refers to hearing "the signal"—that is, the exact words, intonations, and syntax that a speaker uses. Effective listening involves both kinds of processing. As teachers, we may naturally assume that "top-down" processing is more important, but research shows that skills in bottom-up processing is *a key determiner of progress* in L2 listening.

Step 5: Talk about the Topic *Estimated Time: 15 min* Here students gain valuable discussion skills as they talk about the lecture. Discussion skills are an important part of academic success, and most students benefit from structured practice. In these activities, students listen to a short "model discussion" involving both native and non-native speakers, and identify the speaking strategies and gambits that are used. They then attempt to use some of those strategies in their own discussion groups.

Basic Procedure:

- Have students close their books and listen to the discussion.
- With books open, students may listen again and complete Parts A and B to show a basic understanding of the discussion. Alternatively, you can have students answer general comprehension questions: What was this discussion about? What happened in this discussion? etc.

- Next, have students work in groups of three to five, ideally. They should choose a topic and discuss. They should try to use the discussion strategies they have learned in this or previous units.

Methodology Focus: The first two activities in this section are awareness-raising: We want students to understand the content of the discussion *and* try to identify the types of "discourse strategies" that the study group students are using to make the discussion go well. Discussion ability involves a combination of verbal and nonverbal skills. If showing the video, encourage students to focus on the nonverbal actions of the student speakers: their body language (posture), gaze (direction of eyes on other speakers), and back-channeling (signals to show they are paying attention). Speaking strategies develop incrementally. It's important to have students try out different types of strategies in order to see how they may or may not help students express themselves more fully.

Step 6: Review Your Notes *Estimated Time: 15 minutes* Using notes for review and discussion is an important study skill that is developed in this section. Students are guided in reviewing the content of the unit, clarifying concepts, and preparing for the Unit Test. Incomplete, abbreviated examples of actual notes are provided to help students not only review for the test but also compare and improve their own note-taking skills.

Basic Procedure:

- Have students take out their notes and, with a partner, *take turns* explaining the ideas from the lecture.
- Then have them complete the partial notes.
- Ask if there are any questions about the lecture or anything in their notes. You may wish to preview the Unit Test to be sure that students have discussed the items that will be on it.

Methodology Focus: This section "completes the loop" on note-taking. Research shows that the value of note-taking for memory building is realized primarily when note-takers review their notes and attempt to reconstruct the content. By making explicit statements about the content of the lecture, students are "pushing" their output. They need to use precise grammar and vocabulary in order to articulate their ideas.

Step 7: Take the Unit Test *Estimated Time: 15 minutes* This activity completes the study cycle of the unit: preparation, listening to the lecture, review of content, and assessment. The Unit Test, contained only in this Teacher's Pack, is to be photocopied and distributed by the teacher. Students complete it in class as they listen to the test questions on the audio CD. The *Contemporary Topics* tests are challenging—intended to motivate students to learn the material thoroughly. The format features an answer sheet with choices; the question "stem" is provided on audio only. Test-taking skills include verbatim recall, paraphrasing, inferencing, and synthesizing information from parts of the lecture.

Basic Procedure:

- Optional: Play the lecture once again.
- Pass out a copy of the Unit Test to each student and go over the directions.
- Play the audio for the test one time as students complete the test by circling their answers. You may pause the audio between questions.
- Collect the tests to correct yourself, or have students exchange papers and go over the answers in class. Replay the audio as you go over the correct answers.

Methodology Focus: The tests in *Contemporary Topics* have the question "stem" on audio only—the students can't read it. They have to listen carefully and then choose the correct answer. This format is more challenging than most standardized tests, such as the TOEFL. We chose this challenging format to motivate students to work through the unit diligently and know the content well.

Step 8: Extend the Topic
Estimated time: 20 minutes This final section creates a natural extension of the unit topic to areas that are relevant to students. Students first listen to a supplementary media clip drawn from a variety of interesting genres. Typically, students then have a discussion or prepare a class presentation.

Basic Procedure:

- Choose one of the activities, or more if time permits. Review the steps of the activity together.
- Allow time, if possible, for student presentations.

Methodology Focus: An important aspect of a content-based approach is the application, or follow-up step. This step helps students personalize the content of the unit, choosing to develop topics of personal interest. Allowing time for student research and presentations not only increases interest and involvement in the course, but also allows the teacher an opportunity to give individualized feedback that will help students' progress.

By completing these eight steps, students can develop stronger listening, speaking, and note-taking skills and strategies—thereby becoming more confident and independent learners.

Michael Rost
Series Editor

Multimedia Guidelines: With the DVD, you can play the lecture in different modes: video, video with subtitles, video with Coaching Tips, video with Presentation Points, video with Coaching Tips and subtitles, and video with Coaching Tips and Presentation Points. We do not recommend playing the video with both the Presentation Points and subtitles on.

Note that while the DVD is compatible with most computer media players, for optimum viewing we suggest playing the DVD on a television screen (ideally a wide-screen), using a DVD player.

You can also play the lecture as audio only, using the CD.

We recommend that you play the lecture once in "plain" video mode, then once as audio only. For review, you can play the video again with the Presentation Points and/or Coaching Tips turned on. As another review option, students can watch the subtitled version on their own.

Viewing preferences can be selected under SET UP. Or, with a remote control, subtitles can be activated at any time using the caption button, and Presentation Points can be activated at any time using the angle button.

UNIT OVERVIEW

In this unit, students will work with different concepts related to three interesting archaeological "discoveries": the Khipu from the Peruvian Incan society, Stonehenge in England, and the petroglyphs of Easter Island. The lecture focuses on each of the discoveries and how these discoveries give us a glimpse of the past. Follow-up projects extend the topic to other archaeological artifacts chosen by the student.

Connect to the Topic   page 2

~10 minutes

Students are first introduced to the concept of archaeology through three photos: an archaeological dig, replicas of Easter Island statues, and Stonehenge. The survey questions that follow concern students' interests in travel and history.

Build Your Vocabulary   pages 3–4

~15 minutes

Students study these words and phrases related to the study of archaeology:

ancestors	final	piece of land
ancient	finances	researchers
at Stonehenge	for fun	significant
carved into	important for	significant to
colors of	interested in	structures
consist of	link	used for
fascinating	link us to	

After the Interact with Vocabulary! activity, you may want to have students practice using the boldfaced words with their partners. Knowing collocations can help students expand their vocabularies and increase their fluency.

Focus Your Attention   page 5

~10 minutes

Students learn words and phrases that lecturers use to signal order:

First, I want to talk about . . .   *Finally,*
*My **first** (second, third, etc.) point is . . .*   *In conclusion,*
Next, . . .   *My **last** point is . . .*

Listen to the Lecture   pages 6–7

~30 minutes

Students look at photos of petroglyphs and an abacus and discuss with a partner what they know about the items (Before You Listen). Next, they listen to the unit lecture on archaeological discoveries and fill in blanks for missing main ideas and check the main ideas they hear (Listen for Main Ideas). Then they answer true/false items (Listen for Details). You may want to instruct students to write the corrected false statements at the bottom of the page.
Lecture video time: 5 min. 2 sec.   *Number of episodes: 7*

Talk about the Topic *page 8*   *~20 minutes*

Two students—Molly and Michael—discuss the lecture. Part A focuses on matching these students with comments or ideas from the discussion. In Part B, your students work on these discussion strategies:

- Expressing an opinion: "I think you can learn a lot about ancient society . . . "
- Agreeing: "Yeah, OK, I can see that."

For Part C, students are encouraged to use the discussion strategies they've learned. They may use phrases from the student discussion or come up with their own. Remember, your students can discuss one or more of the topics. Also keep in mind that some students may not have much interest in history and archaeology, while others may have great interest.
Student discussion video time: 57 sec.

Review Your Notes *page 9*   *~15 minutes*

Students focus on reconstructing their notes, paying attention to main ideas and key details.

BONUS ACTIVITY

You can supplement this activity with additional "artifacts" you may own or research. Give students the opportunity to discuss each one and add their opinions about the historical value and the way each can link to the past. They might also report on the artifacts that can be found in their home culture.

Take the Unit Test *Teacher's Pack page 7*   *~15 minutes*

You may want to play the lecture again just before giving the test. You also may want to explain to students that *Khipu* has various pronunciations, including KEE-POO and KIP-OO. Students answer standard test questions about the content of the lecture. Specifically, the test covers the following: the importance of archaeological discoveries, the three discoveries, details of each, and the speaker's advice.

Extend the Topic *page 18*   *~30 minutes*
Note that these activities appear at the end of Unit 1b.

- Listening and Discussion: Students listen to a clip of a mother talking to her son about a trip she took to the archaeological site Newgrange. Students then discuss archaeological discoveries they may have seen or might want to experience in the future.
- Project/Presentation: The unit concludes with a suggestion for ways students might research and then report on a geographic area that interests them.

Focus Your Attention:
Try It Out! *page 5*

Speaker: Today I want to talk about how we know that ancient people lived in these mountains. There are two ways. First, we have found parts of early houses. These houses are very different from today's houses. Second, we have found skeletons—or bones of people—nearby. Again we see a difference: These skeletons are very different from today's skeletons. Now, let's look at . . .

Listen for Main Ideas
and Listen for Details *pages 6–7*

Archaeology lecturer: E1 For me, travel isn't just for fun. I'm an archaeologist, so travel is also an important part of my research. Today, I want to tell you about three of my favorite archaeological discoveries. These discoveries are important for research because they link us to our ancestors. The three discoveries you'll hear about today tell us something about one society's ancient accounting practices, another's ancient rituals, and a third's written language. And these three things are still very important to us today, right? E2 OK. Our first stop'll take us to a site in Caral, Peru, in South America. Here we'll look at a recent discovery about a group of people called the Incas. Why is this site important? Well, it shows us that the Incas were very interested in accounting. Archaeologists have found that the Incas used a very detailed system of colored strings for keeping records, or counting things. They called this system of colored strings "Khipu." That's K-h-i-p-u. E3 The Khipu tells us that the Incas were interested in organizing their world and keeping track of finances or maybe events of some type. We know that this system consisted of different colors and lengths of string, and knots in the strings. Don't you wonder what they were counting? Archaeologists do, too, and they're using computers to try to discover the code—or system—of the Khipu. Funny, isn't it, that we're using computers today to figure out what maybe was a type of computer in the past, for the Incas! E4 Let's make another stop, this time in England. Here we find Stonehenge. Have you heard about Stonehenge? It's a site with a structure. And this site shows us how important ritual was for the people who lived in that area thousands of years ago. What do you think the structure was made of? Well, yes, stones, as the name tells us. These stones are huge, much too heavy for people to lift. We wonder how these ancient people placed the stones in the circle that

forms Stonehenge. Archaeologists believe that Stonehenge was used for ceremonies. The size of Stonehenge tells us that human rituals were significant to these ancient people—just like rituals are important for many people today. E5 Our final stop is Easter Island, a very small piece of land in the Pacific Ocean. Now, this is really interesting. Have you ever wondered how ancient people told stories or passed on their knowledge? One way was the use of petroglyphs, spelled p-e-t-r-o-g-l-y-p-h-s. These are pictures or symbols carved into stone, with a knife or tool. Many of these carved pictures tell us about hunting practices, for example. Others show birds, or birdmen, which tells us that birds were very important to the ancient people of this island. E6 In general, the petroglyphs tell us that these people were interested in three things: one, communicating their ideas and stories; two, learning; and three, recording information. E7 Isn't it interesting how these archaeological discoveries can tell us things about ancient societies? Even thousands of years ago, accounting, rituals, and language were important. So, to review: To see one of the earliest computing systems, you can't miss a trip to Peru to see the Incan Khipu. Interested in human rituals? Make sure you visit Stonehenge. And a trip to Easter Island will show you some fascinating petroglyphs—you really should see this early form of writing. That's all for today. Bon voyage!

Coaching Tips

[1] Note-taking: Organizing main ideas What will you hear about today? If your answer was three archaeological discoveries, you're right! Be ready to listen for three main ideas. You could get ready by numbering your notes like this: [see video for note-taking example]. It's good to leave lots of space between the numbers so that you can note the three ideas and then add some details.

[2] Listening: Listening for order The speaker introduces the first important idea with these words: "Our first stop . . ." These words tell you to listen carefully for the information that follows. They also tell you that you'll probably be making more than one stop, right? Think ahead: How will the speaker signal the next stop? As you hear the name of each stop, it's a good idea to write the name in your notes.

[3] Critical Thinking: Using your imagination The speaker describes Stonehenge. Can you imagine how the people of that time built this structure? How did they move the stones? In your mind, try to imagine how Stonehenge looks. This may help you understand details in the lecture.

[4] Listening: Spelling key terms When a speaker spells a word, that means the word is important to the lecture. So it's a good idea to write that word in your notes. Why do you think the speaker wants you to note what a petroglyph is? Look at your notes: Has the speaker spelled out any other terms in this lecture?

Talk about the Topic *page 8*

Molly: Hey, let's talk about the lecture.

Michael: Yeah, sure. Which discovery did you like the best?

Molly: Oh, Stonehenge was my favorite. I thought it was great!

Michael: Why? Why did you like it?

Molly: I guess because I'm really curious about the ceremonies that they had there.

Michael: Yeah, yeah, that is interesting.

Molly: What about you? What was your favorite discovery?

Michael: I really liked the petroglyphs.

Molly: The petroglyphs? Those carvings?

Michael: Yeah.

Molly: Really? Why?

Michael: I think you can learn a lot about ancient society from them.

Molly: How so? Do you mean, by looking at old pictures and symbols and stuff?

Michael: Exactly. I mean, looking at petroglyphs is almost like reading a history book about that society.

Molly: OK, yeah, I can see that. Anyway, it would be so interesting to visit any of these sites.

Michael: I know. I'm with you on that! I'd love to see them up close.

Take the Unit Test

1. Why are archaeological discoveries important to us? b

2. Where did archaeologists find Khipu? a
3. What were Khipu probably used for? c
4. How are scientists trying to discover more about Khipu? c
5. Where is Stonehenge located? b
6. How was Stonehenge created? a
7. What was the purpose of Stonehenge, according to scientists? c
8. What are petroglyphs? c
9. How did the people of Easter Island tell their stories? a
10. What advice does the speaker give? b

Extend the Topic *page 18*

Note that this activity appears at the end of Unit 1b.

Patrick: Mom, you've traveled a lot. Tell me about an archaeological site that you've visited and found fascinating.

Mom: Well, Patrick, when I was younger, I traveled to Ireland to visit some ancient burial tombs—where people's bodies were put after they died. There's one that's really amazing. It is a huge, round, earth-covered stone structure. The stones around the base are white, and they reflect light. Ancient people might have used it to send messages to gods of some kind.

Patrick: How old is it?

Mom: Probably about five thousand years old. It was also used as a place to bury the dead and to note the change of the seasons.

Patrick: What's it called?

Mom: Newgrange. Maybe we could go there together someday. You know, after you're out of school . . .

ANSWER KEY

Build Your Vocabulary *pages 3–4*

B. 1. d 2. a 3. e 4. b 5. j 6. h 7. i 8. f 9. g 10. c **C. Interact with Vocabulary!** 1. for 2. in 3. of 4. to 5. at 6. for 7. to 8. of 9. into 10. for

Focus Your Attention *page 5*

A. First, Second

Before You Listen *page 6*

The photo on page 6 shows petroglyphs, and the photo on page 7 shows an abacus.

Listen for Main Ideas *page 6*

B. Topic: our ancestors; Main idea 1: Khipu; Main idea 2: Stonehenge; Main idea 3: pictures or symbols **C.** 2, 4, 5

Listen for Details *page 7*

1. T 2. F (South America) 3. T 4. T 5. F (Today, scientists are using computers to understand Khipu.) 6. T 7. T 8. T 9. T 10. F (Khipu and petroglyphs tell us that some ancient people could count and write.)

Talk about the Topic *page 8*

A. 1. Michael, Molly 2. Michael, Molly
3. Michael, Molly **B.** 1. Expressing an opinion
(Note: Molly actually says, "Stonehenge was my
favorite.") 2. Expressing an opinion 3. Agreeing
(Note: Molly actually says, "OK, yeah . . .")
4. Agreeing

Review Your Notes *page 9*

Discovery	Khipu	Stonehenge	petrogylphs
Where found	Peru	England	**Easter Island**
Who used	**Incas**	people of **Stonehenge**	people of Easter Island
Material made of	colored strings and knots	huge stones	**stone**
How used	counting & finances	**ceremonies**	telling stories, history
What it tells us about that society	accounting was important	**rituals** were important	**stories/ history** was important

Take the Unit Test

1. b 2. a 3. c 4. c 5. b 6. a 7. c 8. c 9. a
10. b

Extend the Topic *page 18*

Note that this activity appears at the end of Unit 1b.
A. 1. burial tomb in Ireland

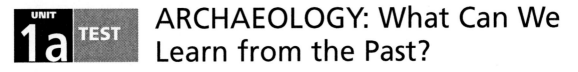

UNIT 1a TEST   ARCHAEOLOGY: What Can We Learn from the Past?

🔊 *Listen to each question. Circle the letter of the correct answer.*

1. a. They tell us how to find archaeological sites.

 b. They teach us about the past.

 c. We can read about archaeological discoveries.

2. a. in Peru

 b. in colorful places

 c. with strings

3. a. to make beautiful pictures

 b. as a place to hide a family's money

 c. to count things

4. a. They are making knots in strings.

 b. They are counting money.

 c. They are using computers.

5. a. in South America

 b. in England

 c. in Peru

6. a. We don't know for certain.

 b. It was used for ceremonies.

 c. People lifted the stones.

7. a. to keep records by counting the stones

 b. to make petroglyphs

 c. to have ceremonies

8. a. huge stones

 b. ancient people

 c. symbols in stone

9. a. They carved pictures or symbols in stone.

 b. They wrote down their stories in books.

 c. They made big circles of stones.

10. a. to take a vacation

 b. to try to see archaeological discoveries

 c. to use new languages to communicate

ARCHAEOLOGY
What Causes a Society to Collapse?

TEACHING TIPS

UNIT OVERVIEW

In this unit, students will examine three societies and the reasons each experienced societal collapse. The lecture focuses on the causes: disease, environmental change, and cultural conflict. Follow-up activities focus on diseases and environmental problems that put cultures in danger.

Connect to the Topic *page 10*   *~10 minutes*

Students are asked to think about the society they live in. They choose statements that describe their society, then compare answers with a partner. Understanding what a society is will help students process what it means for a society to collapse.

Build Your Vocabulary *pages 11–12*   *~15 minutes*

Students study these words and phrases related to societal problems and collapse:

ancient societies	evidence suggests	statues
cultural (beliefs)	go wrong	steal
cultural conflict	a major drop in	steal the riches
cut down trees	population	typical
diseases	major (reason)	typical cause
environment	potential	used up
evidence (of)	potential problem	weapons

The Interact with Vocabulary! activity requires students to listen closely to one another. In addition to circling the Column 2 phrase they hear, students also may want to write the number of the corresponding sentence. This will make checking answers easier. After the Interact with Vocabulary! activity, students may practice the boldfaced collocations with partners.

Focus Your Attention *page 13*   *~10 minutes*

Students learn words and phrases that signal effects and outcomes:

*There are **two (three, many) reasons for** collapse . . .*
*Collapse **is a result of** . . .*
*Collapse **happens because of** . . .*
*Collapse **is caused by** . . .*
*Another **effect of** . . .*

Listen to the Lecture *pages 14–15*   *~30 minutes*

Students think about two situations involving potential societal collapse before listening to the unit lecture about the same three cultures discussed in Unit 1a, but with the focus here on how they collapsed. Students then fill in missing information and check the main ideas of the lecture (Listen for Main Ideas). Next they answer true/false items (Listen for Details).
Lecture video time: 5 min. 38 sec.   Number of episodes: 8

NOTE

Remember that with the DVD, you can play the lecture in different modes: video, video with Presentation Points, video with Coaching Tips, video with subtitles, video with subtitles and Coaching Tips, and video with Coaching Tips and Presentation Points. (We do not recommend playing the video with both the Presentation Points and subtitles on.) You can also play the lecture as audio only, using the CD. We recommend that you play the lecture once in "plain" video mode, then once as audio only. For review, you can play the video again with the Presentation Points and/or Coaching Tips turned on. As another review option, students can watch the subtitled version on their own.

Talk about the Topic *page 16*   *~20 minutes*

Two students—Rob and Hannah—discuss the lecture. Part A focuses on matching these students with comments or ideas from the discussion. In Part B, your students work on these discussion strategies:

- Expressing an opinion: "Well, personally, I think . . . "
- Agreeing: "Well, I agree that . . . "
- Disagreeing: "But I don't really believe . . . "

For Part C, students are encouraged to use the discussion strategies they've learned. They may use phrases from the student discussion and/or the Discussion Strategy box, or come up with their own. Remember, your students may have some interesting ideas about how to avoid societal collapse.
Student discussion video time: 1 min. 51 sec.

Review Your Notes *page 17*   *~15 minutes*

Students focus on reconstructing their notes, discussing the causes and effects they've noted.

BONUS ACTIVITY

You can supplement this activity with information you or your students may know about other societies that have collapsed or have come close to collapsing.

Take the Unit Test *Teacher's Pack page 13*   *~15 minutes*

You may want to play the lecture again just before giving the test. Students answer standard test questions about the content of the lecture. Specifically, the test covers the following: what happened to the three societies, what the causes of collapse were, details of the cause of each collapse, and what the speaker asked students to think about.

Extend the Topic *page 19*   *~30 minutes*

- Listening and Discussion: Students listen to and discuss a clip about environmental problems and possible results.
- Project/Presentation: Students conduct library or Internet research on a disease and how it might affect society today. They discuss their findings in a small group setting while other group members take notes.

Focus Your Attention:
Try It Out! *page 13*

Speaker: So the people cut down all of the trees. Well, what happened when the people cut down all of the trees? They disappeared! They died. Why? There are two main reasons. One result of cutting down the trees was that there was no wood left for making farming tools. And without farming tools you have no food. Another effect of cutting down the trees is they had nothing to build houses with. And without homes, they became cold and sick. So these are two main reasons why these people disappeared. OK, any questions so far? . . .

Listen for Main Ideas and Listen for Details *pages 14–15*

Archaeology lecturer: E1 Last time, we talked about archaeological discoveries and what they tell us about ancient societies. So what happened to those three societies we discussed last time? Remember? The Incas of South America? The people of Easter Island? And the people of Stonehenge? What made these societies collapse, or disappear? E2 Well, today, I want to talk about that, about why these three societies died out. Why did they collapse? Generally speaking, there are three different reasons: disease, environmental problems, and cultural conflict. OK, let me repeat that . . . the three different reasons why these societies collapsed are disease, environmental problems, and cultural conflict. And I want you to understand: These three reasons are also typical causes of societal collapse throughout history. And that may have significant meaning for us today. More on that later . . . E3 OK, let's get started on the three reasons. First, we have disease. Of course, diseases can kill people, right? But a whole society? Our first example describes how the Incan society of Peru disappeared. Evidence suggests that disease was the cause. Five hundred years ago, the Incan Empire was the largest empire in the world with 10 million people. And it was also the richest. And these riches—consisting of gold and valuable stones, for example—led to this great society's disappearance. E4 How? Well, when the Europeans heard about the Incas' wealth, they wanted it—they wanted all of it. So they traveled to the Incan empire to steal the riches. And while they were in the Americas, they passed new diseases to the Incan people. One of the most deadly diseases was smallpox. Nearly two-thirds of the Incas died because they got smallpox. So disease caused the Incan empire to collapse. And, historically, disease is a big reason why many other societies have collapsed. E5 Now, the second cause of societal collapse I want to discuss is environmental change. An example of collapse due to environmental change is Easter Island, in the Pacific Ocean. Environmental change can be caused by nature, or it can be caused by humans. In the case of Easter Island, research suggests it was caused by people. E6 About 1,200 years ago, the first people of Easter Island cut down all the trees on the island. They used the trees as rollers to move their statues. Can you guess what went wrong? Easter Island soon had major problems because the people had used up all of the trees! Without trees, they couldn't build boats for fishing or make tools for farming. The shortage of trees led to a major drop in population. We might say that the Easter Islanders disappeared because they couldn't live in this new environment—this environment without trees. A very sad story, isn't it? E7 The third and final big reason societies collapse is cultural conflict. Archaeologists have found evidence that the ancient people of Stonehenge were very peaceful for a time. They had no weapons except for hunting. However, later, they began to make weapons of war. Their culture changed from a very peaceful one to a culture of war and fighting. Archaeologists believe that the people of Stonehenge also began to fight within their culture. And soon this society collapsed. Why? Because they experienced cultural conflict. E8 OK, so remember: Historically, the three big reasons why societies have collapsed are disease, environmental change, and cultural conflict. For next time, I want you to think about these three causes of collapse. Then think about problems in the world today . . . Which societies are strong, and which face potential collapse? I'll see you the next class.

Coaching Tips

[1] Listening: Identifying cause and effect The speaker says the lecture will be about why these three societies died out, or collapsed. When he says the word *why*, he means that there are reasons, or causes. The speaker will explain these reasons. As you listen to the rest of this lecture, you'll hear other words signaling cause and effect, including *cause*, *caused by*, and *reason*.

[2] Note-taking: Noting cause and effect Did you get the first reason? You might want to write the number *1* in your notes and then write the reason: disease. For example, your notes might look something like this: [see video for note-taking example].

[3] Critical Thinking: Guessing The speaker says that humans caused the environment on Easter Island to change. Can you guess what the environmental change was? What about how the people caused it? Write down your guesses. Guessing helps you get ready for the next part of the lecture. After you hear the lecturer talk about environmental change, check to see if your guesses were close.

[4] Critical Thinking: Thinking of examples In his lecture, the speaker gives three reasons for societal collapse. Then he gives an example for each reason. Can you think of any other examples of societal collapse from disease, environmental change, or cultural conflict? Maybe you know about another society from history. It can be helpful to think of your own examples—and add them to your notes.

Talk about the Topic *page 16*

Hannah: So, are you ready to talk about the lecture?

Rob: Yeah. So, um, I have a question or maybe it's just a comment.

Hannah: Go ahead. What is it?

Rob: You know how the speaker was asking us to think about problems in the world today?

Hannah: Yeah—what kind of problems were you thinking about?

Rob: Well, personally, I think maybe cultural conflict will be the cause of the next societal collapse.

Hannah: You think so? Cultural conflict?

Rob: Yeah. With all the fighting and the wars going on, like between people of different cultures.

Hannah: Hmm. Well, I agree that there is a lot of conflict in the world today.

Rob: Exactly.

Hannah: But I don't really believe that any society is going to *totally* disappear. Do you?

Rob: Yeah, I think it's possible. I mean, just turn on the TV news!

Hannah: Well, in my opinion, I say environment is our most serious problem. If we're not careful, a lot of societies could disappear.

Rob: Hmm. That's a good point. I hear what you're saying. But don't you think that we're working to make the environment better?

Hannah: Well, I agree that we're trying. Yeah, you're right: People are becoming more and more "green," I guess.

Rob: And healthier.

Hannah: Right. Well, how about disease as a cause of society collapsing. Can you see that happening?

Rob: No, not with modern medicine. You?

Hannah: I agree. I can't really see disease causing a society to die out.

Rob: Still, I say that we always have to remember the lessons of history.

Hannah: Yeah, I agree.

Take the Unit Test

1. What happened to the Incas, the people of Easter Island, and the people of Stonehenge?
2. Which is *not* a reason for societal collapse?
3. How many people lived in the Incan Empire?
4. Why did Europeans travel to Peru?
5. Why did the Incan Empire collapse?
6. The speaker gave two causes of change in the environment. What are they?
7. Why did the people of Easter Island cut down the trees?
8. What happened on Easter Island after the trees were cut down?
9. How did the culture of Stonehenge change?
10. What does the speaker ask you to think about?

Extend the Topic *page 19*

Reporter: Hi, ladies. Can I interrupt your lunch here on the campus lawn for an interview for the campus radio show "What's on Your Mind?"

Melinda: Sure.

Zoe: No problem.

Reporter: So, talk to me—what's on your minds?

Zoe: Well, Melinda and I were just talking about all of the problems with the environment. It's scary!

Melinda: Yeah. I'm an environmental education major, and so I was saying to Zoe how we need to face the fact that we're living in a time of environmental change.

Zoe: But here's my question: Do they know what's causing the change? I mean, is it because the temperature is rising?

Melinda: Well, there are different ideas out there. But I believe that's it exactly. With even small increases in temperatures, there can be major changes in our environment. For example, as it gets warmer, the ice caps melt. When that happens, the oceans rise.

Zoe: Oh. And when that happens, water covers more land, right?

Melinda: Right. In the future, people who live near the ocean may have to move—or they might not have a home! And think about how many people that might affect!

Reporter: Very interesting. Thanks for sharing . . .

ANSWER KEY

Build Your Vocabulary *pages 11–12*

B. 1. a 2. b 3. a 4. c 5. a 6. b 7. b 8. a 9. b
10. a **C. Interact with Vocabulary!** 1. d 2. h 3. i
4. a 5. c 6. g 7. e 8. b 9. f 10. j

Focus Your Attention *page 13*

A. Words the speaker uses to signal effect/outcome:
what happened, two main reasons, One result of,
another effect of, two main reasons why

Listen for Main Ideas *pages 14–15*

B. Topic: collapse; Main idea 1: Disease; Main idea
2: environmental; Main idea 3: Cultural conflict;
C. 2, 4, 6 (Note: While item 3 is true, it isn't a main
idea.)

Listen for Details *page 15*

B. 1. F (many societies have) 2. T 3. T 4. F (stole
the Incas' riches) 5. T 6. T 7. F (did need) 8. T
9. T 10. T

Talk about the Topic *page 16*

A. 1. Rob and Hannah 2. Hannah 3. Hannah
B. 1. Expressing an opinion 2. Agreeing
3. Expressing an opinion and / or disagreeing
4. Disagreeing

Review Your Notes *page 17*

Society that collapsed ↓	Cause	Effect
Incan Empire	Europeans wanted Incan riches	took riches and brought **disease**
Easter Island	people cut down **trees**	couldn't build **boats** or make tools
Society at Stonehenge	people began making **weapons**	changed from peaceful to culture of war and **fighting**

Take the Unit Test

1. c 2. b 3. a 4. b 5. a 6. c 7. a 8. b 9. b
10. b

Extend the Topic *page 19*

C. 1. environmental change

UNIT 1b TEST — ARCHAEOLOGY: What Causes a Society to Collapse?

Listen to each question. Circle the letter of the correct answer.

1. a. They shared their wealth with others.
   b. They are ancient societies.
   c. Their societies died out.

2. a. disease
   b. statues
   c. environmental changes

3. a. 10 million
   b. 10 billion
   c. 500

4. a. They wanted to make people sick.
   b. They wanted riches.
   c. They wanted to make weapons.

5. a. because of smallpox
   b. because of trees
   c. both a and b

6. a. gold and people
   b. nature and disease
   c. people and nature

7. a. because they needed the trees to roll their statues
   b. because they wanted to use the trees for fishing
   c. because they didn't want the trees on the island

8. a. It wasn't pretty anymore.
   b. The population dropped.
   c. The fish died.

9. a. The people wanted peace.
   b. The people began to fight each other.
   c. The stones fell down.

10. a. using trees for building
    b. which societies today might collapse
    c. how to get rich

ANTHROPOLOGY
Culture Shock

UNIT OVERVIEW

In this unit, students will explore the concepts of culture shock and the cultural adjustment process. The lecture focuses on culture shock: its definition, its four stages, and the characteristics of each stage, including the primary symptoms and the duration. Follow-up projects extend the topic to students' and others' experiences with other cultures.

Connect to the Topic *page 20*   *~10 minutes*

Students take a survey about their cultural experiences. Survey questions concern students' cross-cultural interests, opinions, and experiences.

Build Your Vocabulary *pages 21–22*   *~15 minutes*

Students study these words and phrases related to the study of anthropology and culture shock:

(a big) adjustment	got used to	push away
(felt) anxious	heard of	reject
away from home	normal	similar
behavior	on time	symptoms
customs	process	views of the world
excitement		

After the Interact with Vocabulary! activity, you may want to have students practice using the boldfaced words with their partners. Knowing collocations can help students expand their vocabularies and increase their fluency.

Focus Your Attention *page 23*   *~10 minutes*

Students learn cues that lecturers use when introducing details:

What do you think happens in . . .
So, what can we say about . . . ⎫
What have you heard about . . . . ⎬ *culture shock?*
What do we know about . . . ⎭

Listen to the Lecture *pages 24–25*   *~30 minutes*

Students discuss a situation involving culture shock (Before You Listen) before listening to the unit lecture on culture shock. Students then check from a list the main ideas they hear (Listen for Main Ideas). Next they answer multiple-choice questions (Listen for Details). *Lecture video time: 5 min. 25 sec.*   *Number of episodes: 9*

Talk about the Topic *page 26* ~*20 minutes*

Two students—Michael and May—discuss the lecture. Part A focuses on matching these students with comments or ideas from the discussion. In Part B, your students work on these discussion strategies:

- Asking for opinions or ideas: "What's your experience here been like?"
- Asking for clarification or confirmation: "How do you know?"

For Part C, students are encouraged to use the discussion strategies they've learned. They may use phrases from the student discussion and/or the Discussion Strategy box, or come up with their own. Keep in mind that some students may be reluctant to talk about their personal experiences and feelings, while others will want to do so with great enthusiasm.
Student discussion video time: 1 min. 32 sec.

Review Your Notes *page 27* ~*15 minutes*

Students focus on reconstructing their notes, paying attention to main ideas and key details.

BONUS ACTIVITY

You can supplement this activity with a discussion of different cultural traditions, practices, behaviors, and beliefs associated with common life events. Such events include leaving home to study at a school, attending social activities, dating, marriage, and the birth of a child. You may want to remind students that each region and each family will have its own cultural behaviors and beliefs. Provide students with an opportunity to compare and contrast their cultural practices.

Take the Unit Test *Teacher's Pack page 19* ~*15 minutes*

You may want to play the lecture again just before giving the test. Students answer standard test questions about the content of the lecture. Specifically, the test covers the following: cause of culture shock, characteristics of each culture shock stage, and duration of culture shock stages.

Extend the Topic *pages 36–37* ~*30 minutes*
Note that these activities appear at the end of Unit 2b.

- Listening and Discussion: Students listen to and discuss a chat between two students about their first day of classes.
- Project/Presentation: Students interview someone about his or her cross-cultural experience. Then they share their findings in small groups.

Focus Your Attention:
Try It Out! *page 23*

Speaker: Now, to the next stage: the Acceptance Stage. What do you think happens in the Acceptance Stage of culture shock? Yes, of course, "acceptance" means you start to like some of the customs or practices of the new culture. You also begin to accept some of the ways people act. You know, maybe the people stop to talk with their neighbors every day, and you learn to like that tradition. What else can we say about the Acceptance Stage? Well, you also begin to feel more comfortable because you can speak the language better and do things like talk to neighbors or explain an illness to a doctor.

Listen for Main Ideas and Listen for Details *pages 24–25*

Anthropology lecturer: E1 Today we're going to discuss what it's like to live in a new culture, a new society. Now, as you may know, the study of culture and society is called anthropology. Well, I became interested in anthropology when I was nineteen and traveled to the country of Albania. It was my first time living away from home. And it really changed my view of the world and of myself. E2 So what happened to me when I was in this new culture? Can you guess? I experienced culture shock. Now have you heard of culture shock? No? OK, well, some of you may have it right now! OK, don't worry; it's not an illness. It's the shock, or the surprising feelings you have when you enter another culture. Culture shock often happens to people when they leave their home culture and go to live in a different culture, which we call the "host culture." Culture shock is a process. That is, research shows that culture shock has four stages. So let's look at these four stages of adjustment—or getting used to a new culture. E3 The first stage is called the Excitement Stage. Now this stage usually starts before you even leave your home culture—also called your "native culture." Now before I left home, I was certain that my life was going to be completely wonderful when I finally reached Albania. Have any of you had similar experiences? So you can understand why this first stage is called the Excitement Stage. And this excitement continues until after you enter the host culture. Now all the new sights and sounds and smells and tastes are very interesting when you first arrive. And, in fact, this stage may last anywhere from a few days to six months. E4 Well, after some weeks, your feelings change—oh yes, you begin to have very different feelings. You move from the Excitement Stage to the second stage of culture shock, called the Rejection Stage. Why is it called that? Well, because you reject, or push away, the host culture. The main symptom is that you don't feel like participating in this new culture. In my case, I realized I was very different from the people around me. And I felt unhappy that I couldn't fit in. I wanted to go home immediately. Right away. E5 Now this feeling's normal. When you're living in another culture, the language is difficult. And people's behaviors—you know, how they act—they can seem strange. For example, I came to class on time every day. But some students came in fifteen, even thirty minutes late. And the teacher never seemed to mind. I couldn't understand this. E6 There are other symptoms of the Rejection Stage. You might feel tired or anxious. Things that felt simple to do back home, now, in this new environment, feel like a lot of work: like answering the phone or shopping. And then there's loneliness. Me, I really missed my family—and especially my mom's peach pie. Anyway, so that's the Rejection Stage. And how long it lasts varies from one to six months. E7 Well, fortunately, most people move on from the Rejection Stage, and they enter the third stage: the Acceptance Stage. What do you think happens in this stage? Right, of course: You begin to accept some of the behaviors and the beliefs of the host culture. Life becomes easier: Your language skills get better. And you understand the behaviors and the customs around you. For example, I learned to understand my teacher's way of thinking, and stopped caring when other students were late for class. This is normal in the Acceptance Stage: You learn that the host culture isn't better or worse than your home culture—just different. E8 And that brings us to the fourth and final stage of cultural adjustment: Acculturation. That's a-c-c-u-l-t-u-r-a-t-i-o-n. Now, to become acculturated means to become adjusted to the culture. And this happens after living in a place for several years. In this stage, you enjoy many of the customs and the beliefs of the host culture, but you still keep your home culture. E9 OK, time's almost up so let's review. Today, we talked about the four stages of culture shock: Excitement, Rejection, Acceptance, and Acculturation. And we covered some of the characteristics of each. Now for next time, be ready to discuss any experiences you may have had with these stages of cultural adjustment.

Coaching Tips

[1] Critical Thinking: Thinking of examples The speaker tells about his visit to Albania. This is his example. Do you have an example of a trip you've taken to another culture? Maybe your example is like the speaker's. Or maybe it's different. Thinking about your experience can help you to understand the lecture better.

[2] Listening: Listening for order signals The speaker says culture shock has four stages. Then he uses a signal phrase to give the first stage. He says, "The first stage is called the Excitement Stage." What signal phrase did you hear? By saying "the first stage," the speaker is signaling the first main idea of his lecture. When you hear this kind of signal phrase again, you'll know that you're going to hear another stage.

[3] Listening: Listening for details "What do you think happens in this stage?" the speaker asks. This is a linking question. Speakers may use linking questions to signal they're about to give important details about the main idea. When you hear a linking question, be ready to listen for details. It's a good idea to write these details in your notes.

[4] Critical Thinking: Predicting The speaker says, "Be ready to discuss any experiences you may have had with . . . cultural adjustment." Based on that statement, can you predict what will happen in the next class? One possibility is that he'll ask students to give personal examples of adjusting to a new culture. When speakers hint at what they're planning for the next class, they're giving you a chance to prepare.

Talk about the Topic   *page 26*

May: Ready to go over the culture shock notes?

Michael: Yeah, I'm really glad we're going over these together. I think I missed one of the stages. There are four, right?

May: Yeah, that's what I have. It's Excitement first, and then Rejection . . .

Michael: Yup. Then Acceptance third.

May: Right. So, Excitement, Rejection, and Acceptance.

Michael: That stage feels so good!

May: How do you know?

Michael: Well, in high school I spent a year living in Sapporo, Japan.

May: No way! That's so cool. Wait, where's Sa- Sap-

Michael: Sapporo.

May: Yeah, I've heard about that. It's in the north, right?

Michael: Right. It snowed so much the winter that I was there. And that's actually what helped me.

May: What do you mean?

Michael: Well, I love to ski, and so I ended up making two really good Japanese friends through skiing.

May: Hmm, so that's how you began to accept the culture?

Michael: Exactly. Well, what about you? What's your experience here been like?

May: Well, I feel like I've passed through all four stages by now.

Michael: Oh, that's the one I missed, the fourth one. What is it?

May: It's Acculturation. Yeah. I can truthfully say that I'm acculturated. I enjoy the host culture, but, I mean, I still keep my home culture right here.

Michael: Well, that's great. I mean, it must've been hard at first to get acculturated.

Take the Unit Test

1. What is the cause of culture shock?
2. Which one is *not* true about people who have culture shock?
3. When does the Excitement Stage of culture shock usually begin?
4. How long does the Excitement Stage last?
5. Which stage comes after the Excitement Stage?
6. How do people in the Rejection Stage feel? Choose *two* answers.
7. What does a person in the Acceptance Stage learn?
8. Which is *not* a reason that people feel happier in the Acceptance Stage?
9. When does the Acculturation Stage happen?
10. What do people in the Acculturation Stage like about the host culture?

Extend the Topic   *page 36*

Note that this activity appears at the end of Unit 2b.

Klaus: Gosh, I'm tired. The first day of classes are so busy! But hey, Ibrahim, listen to what happened in my economics course today. The professor, Dr. Johnson, walked into the room and introduced herself as "Sarah Johnson." Then she said, "You can call me Sarah." Can you believe it?

Ibrahim: Hey, that same thing happened in my Biology 101 class this morning. The professor walked in the room and told us to call him "Tom." Klaus, I almost fell off my chair. The man has written three books, and he tells students to call him "Tom." In my country, we always say "Professor" or "Doctor."

Klaus: Yeah, we do the same thing in my country. I can't call my professor "Sarah"!

Ibrahim: Do you know something else that's different, Klaus? This morning, our professor asked us to introduce ourselves and tell him why we're interested in studying business. That's something that doesn't happen at home. I'm not sure I like how personal that feels.

Klaus: Well, I think professors here want to get to know their students.
Ibrahim: Maybe. I guess there are more differences than we first thought. Hey, there's Yuri. Let's ask her what happened in her chemistry class this morning . . .

ANSWER KEY

Build Your Vocabulary *pages 21–22*

B. 1. process 2. similar 3. normal 4. custom 5. anxious 6. adjustment 7. rejects 8. excitement 9. symptom 10. behavior **C. Interact with Vocabulary!** 1. away 2. on 3. to 4. of 5. of 6. away

Focus Your Attention *page 23*

A. 1. What do you think happens in the Acceptance Stage of culture shock? 2. What else can we say about the Acceptance Stage? C. The quotation symbol is used to indicate that the same information repeats.

Listen for Main Ideas *page 24*

B. 1, 3, 5, 6

Listen for Details *page 25*

B. 1. b 2. a 3. a 4. b 5. b 6. b 7. b 8. a

Talk about the Topic *page 26*

A. 1. Michael 2. Michael 3. May B. 1. Asking for clarification or confirmation 2. Asking for clarification or confirmation (Note: May actually says, "It's," not "That's.") 3. Asking for clarification or confirmation 4. Asking for opinions or ideas

Review Your Notes *page 27*

Culture Shock				
	Stage 1	Stage 2	Stage 3	Stage 4
Name:	Excitement	**Rejection**	Acceptance	Acculturation
Details: • starts:	before leaving home	**after some weeks**	after 6 months	**after several years**
• description of feelings:	**excitement**	**don't want to be in new culture; tired, anxious, lonely**	accept some behaviors & beliefs	**enjoy customs & beliefs**
• lasts:	**few days- several months**	**1–6 months**	several years	—
Ex. from lecture or own experience	Life is wonderful.	**students late for class** **(or missed family & peach pie)**	understood teacher's way of thinking	**enjoy host culture & keep home culture**

Take the Unit Test

1. b 2. c 3. a 4. c 5. a 6. a and c 7. c 8. b 9. b 10. c

Extend the Topic *page 36*

Note that this activity appears at the end of Unit 2b.
A. 1. How to address professors—formality/informality

 **TEST** ANTHROPOLOGY: Culture Shock

Listen to each question. Circle the letter of the correct answer.

1. a. an illness
   b. a move into a different culture
   c. a bad experience

2. a. Many things are new to them.
   b. They are living in a host culture.
   c. They are unhappy every day.

3. a. before a person leaves home
   b. after a person moves into the host culture
   c. after a person sees new places

4. a. one day
   b. six months to a year
   c. from a few days to six months

5. a. the Rejection Stage
   b. the Acceptance Stage
   c. the Acculturation Stage

6. a. anxious
   b. excited
   c. tired

7. a. The host culture is better than the home culture.
   b. The host culture is worse than the home culture.
   c. The host culture is different from the home culture.

8. a. They have better language skills.
   b. They eat better food.
   c. They have a better understanding of behaviors and customs.

9. a. after living in the host culture for six months
   b. after living in the host culture for several years
   c. after leaving the host culture

10. a. some customs
    b. some beliefs
    c. both a and b

UNIT 2b ANTHROPOLOGY
Third Culture Kids

TEACHING TIPS

UNIT OVERVIEW

In this unit, students will learn about different concepts related to the development of children growing up in a third culture—that is, a culture containing elements of both their native and their host cultures. The lecture focuses on third culture kids (known as TCKs): the definition of third culture children, and the benefits and challenges of being a third culture kid. Follow-up projects extend the topic to the lifelong effects of being a third culture kid.

Connect to the Topic *page 28* ~10 minutes

Students take a survey about culture and its impact on their lives. Survey questions ask students to reflect on their personal experiences and attitudes toward intercultural relationships and living in another culture.

Build Your Vocabulary *pages 29–30* ~15 minutes

Students study these words and phrases related to the study of anthropology and TCKs:

comfortable	lifestyle	source (of)
the definition of	live in a culture	tradition
the first time	a mixture of	the traditions
flexible	participate (in)	followed
growing up	relate to	unsure
identity	some traditions for	the values of

The Interact with Vocabulary! activity remind students that they must choose the correct word to make the phrase complete. For example, in item 1, they must choose between *a* and *the* (the correct answer being *a mixture of*). For the Interact with Vocabulary! activity, you may want to encourage students to first notice the boldfaced words and explain that the boldfaced words form collocations when paired correctly.

Focus Your Attention *page 31* ~10 minutes

Students learn cues that lecturers use when introducing new vocabulary and their definitions:

*Culture **means** . . .*   *Culture, **that is** . . .*
*Culture, **or** . . .*   *Culture, **also called** . . .*

Listen to the Lecture *pages 32–33* ~30 minutes

Students read about a Japanese girl's experience living in Russia (Before You Listen) before listening to the unit lecture on third culture kids. Students then complete an outline and identify the lecture's main ideas (Listen for Main Ideas). Next they answer multiple-choice items (Listen for Details).
Lecture video time: 5 min. 7 sec.   Number of episodes: 8

Talk about the Topic *page 34* *~20 minutes*

Two students—Molly and Rob—discuss the lecture. Part A focuses on matching these students with comments or ideas from the discussion. In Part B, your students work on these discussion strategies:

- Expressing an opinion: "I guess it's exciting to be a TCK . . ."
- Disagreeing: "A lot of people think that. But . . ."
- Asking for clarification or confirmation: "Then, I guess you didn't agree with everything?"

For Part C, students are encouraged to use the discussion strategies they've learned. They may use phrases from the student discussion and/or the Discussion Strategy box, or come up with their own. Keep in mind that some students may be reluctant to talk about their personal experiences, feelings, and opinions, while others may feel quite comfortable sharing memories, ideas, and views.
Student discussion video time: 1 min. 24 sec.

Review Your Notes *page 35* *~15 minutes*

Students focus on reconstructing their notes, paying attention to definitions and key details.

Take the Unit Test *Teacher's Pack page 25* *~15 minutes*

You may want to play the lecture again just before giving the test. Students answer standard test questions about the content of the lecture. Specifically, the test covers the following: definition of a third culture kid, benefits of being a TCK, characteristics of TCKs, and challenges of TCKs.

Extend the Topic *page 37* *~30 minutes*

- Listening and Discussion: Students listen to and discuss an anthropologist's research on adult TCKs. The anthropologist details how adult TCKs can be helped and hindered by the childhood cross-cultural experiences.
- Project/Presentation: This unit concludes with students researching a TCK and sharing their findings in small groups.

Focus Your Attention: Try It Out! *page 31*

Speaker: Third culture kids differ from other kids in many ways. One is environment—that is, where they live. They live in a culture different from their parents' culture. Another difference is their identity. Identity means who they are. Third culture kids see themselves as a mix of at least two cultures, not just one. Additionally, they are often very flexible, or able to change how they think and act. OK, so those are three differences . . .

Listen for Main Ideas and Listen for Details *pages 32–33*

Anthropology lecturer: E1 Well, last time, we talked about the stages of culture shock. And I shared my experience of living and studying in Albania. Today, I'd like to talk about another subject from anthropology—it's called third culture kids. As you may know, many anthropologists study other cultures by living in them. This means that their children often are "third culture kids," or T-C-Ks, for short. E2 Now what exactly do I mean by "third culture kids"? Well, let's see if we can find a definition by looking at my own three kids' experience. Our family lived in Ghana, Africa, for seven years. Of course, in our home, my kids learned the behaviors and values of the American culture because my wife and I are American. But at the same time, our kids were also learning about the Ghanaian culture from their Ghanaian friends and neighbors. The kids also attended an international school which had children from several different cultures. So that was another source of learning. So "third culture kids" are children who grow up in a culture different from their parents' native culture. While participating in this new lifestyle, these children are also learning about their own identity. That is, they're learning about themselves and the world around them. E3 For example, as young children, my kids celebrated Thanksgiving and learned to enjoy jazz music—American traditions. At the same time, they were also celebrating the Ghanaian independence day on July first and were listening to West African "highlife" music whenever they were with their Ghanaian friends. So they grew up learning behaviors and beliefs of both their home culture and their host culture. That is, they grew up in an environment that was a mixture of two cultures—so it was really like a new, different culture: a "third culture." E4 Now, is being a TCK a good thing? Well, it can be helpful to children in a number of ways. Here are four of the most important. First, these kids become interested in and learn to accept other cultures. Second, they learn to be flexible—they live happily and successfully in different cultures. Third, TCKs learn to make friends quickly, and they often have a large circle of friends all over the world. And, finally, of course, these kids have excellent communication skills in several languages. E5 However, third culture kids also have some problems that other kids don't. For one, because they grow up in this special, third culture, they often don't feel like they really belong in either their home culture or their host culture. So, they're a little unsure about their identity. For example, even though our family has been back in the U.S. for several years now, my kids still don't completely think of themselves as American. And they don't think of themselves as Ghanaian either. My son says he is a nomad—you know, someone who lives in many places but doesn't really have a home. E6 Another problem for third culture kids is that they may not feel socially comfortable with their relatives. Why is this? Because they've never really spent much time with them. Similarly, TCKs may not "click" with or relate well to other American kids. Often it's because they haven't experienced the same cultural events in their lives. For example, like seeing popular movies or big sports events. Actually, third culture kids often say they're most comfortable when they're with other TCKs. That's easy to understand, isn't it? E7 The third and final problem for third culture kids is that they don't have much experience making deep, long-lasting friendships. This is because they know that they'll be leaving the host culture at some time. And, if they're at an international school, their friends are always coming and going, too. E8 OK, let's end here by saying that third culture kids can understand and adjust to other ways of life and other languages, but they may not feel completely comfortable in any one culture. However, if you ask my kids, they'll tell you that they really enjoyed growing up as TCKs—and as a parent, I'm glad they did, too!

Coaching Tips

[1] **Critical Thinking: Inferencing** What is the speaker's job? Does he say? He says that many anthropologists study other cultures by living in them. Then he adds that he's going to use his own family's experience of living in Africa as an example for today's lecture on third culture kids. From this information, you can infer two things: that he's an anthropologist, and that his kids are third culture kids. By putting bits of information together, you can make an inference—and understand even more than what a speaker tells you directly.

[2] Note-taking: Listing items How many items are you about to hear? The speaker gives you the number—four—ahead of time. With this information, you can prepare your notes. It's a good idea to make a list in your notes so that you can write down the details as the speaker gives them. Your notes might look like this: [see video for note-taking example].

[3] Note-taking and Listening: Definitions The speaker says that "TCKs may not click with or relate well to other American kids." Did you hear a new phrase here? Do you know the meaning of the phrase "click with"? The speaker gives the definition of this phrase by adding "or relate well to." After giving a new term, speakers will often follow with a different term that has a similar meaning, to help you understand. The equal sign is one way to show a definition. Your notes might look like this: [see video for note-taking example].

[4] Critical Thinking: Responding to a topic Now that you understand what it means to be a TCK, what do you think about the life of third culture kids? Why do you think the speaker is glad his kids grew up as TCKs? What about all of the problems TCKs have? It's a good idea to consider your own feelings about a topic as you review your notes.

Talk about the Topic *page 34*

Molly: So, I bet that lecture was pretty interesting to you, huh?

Rob: You mean because I'm a former TCK?

Molly: Uh-huh.

Rob: Yeah, it feels good to be understood!

Molly: I bet.

Rob: You know, I could identify with almost everything that the lecturer described.

Molly: Oh, well, then, I guess you didn't agree with everything?

Rob: Well, the only thing that I didn't agree with was the part about relatives, about not being comfortable with your relatives.

Molly: Isn't that a problem for you? Are you close to your relatives?

Rob: I am, yeah. Well, even though I didn't get to see them very often growing up, whenever we were together, we were just happy to see each other. So, I think in that way, the distance made us closer.

Molly: That's a good point. I guess it's exciting to be a TCK.

Rob: Well, a lot of people think that. But it's not always easy.

Molly: No?

Rob: No, I mean, for me, my family moved, like, every two years. So I was really a "nomad."

Molly: A nomad, huh? You mean because you never felt like you had a permanent home?

Rob: Right.

Molly: Hmm.

Rob: And now, when people ask me, like, "Where are you from?" I don't know what to say!

Molly: Maybe you should say a different country every time just to keep the conversation interesting.

Rob: I like that. I think I'll do that from now on.

Molly: Uh-huh.

Take the Unit Test

1. How do many anthropologists study other cultures?
2. Who are third culture kids?
3. What did the speaker's children learn in Ghana, Africa?
4. What do third culture kids learn? Choose *two* answers.
5. What do third culture kids often *not* have?
6. What is often a problem for third culture kids?
7. Why does the speaker's son say he is a nomad?
8. Why do third culture kids have fewer deep friendships?
9. Who are third culture kids often friends with?
10. How do the speaker's children feel about growing up as TCKs?

Extend the Topic *page 37*

Interviewer: Dr. Paul, first of all, when did you start to study TCKs?

Dr. Paul: Well we started about twenty years ago, so we now have a lot of information.

Interviewer: OK, so what are some of the most important things you learned in your study?

Dr. Paul: First, we know that many adult TCKs are doing just fine. Many of them are living happily and using their international experience in professions such as medicine, education, business, journalism, and politics. These are positions in which these adult TCKs meet people from many different cultures.

Interviewer: Are there adult TCKs who are not doing as well?

Dr. Paul: Yes, of course. Some adult TCKs are angry because they feel like they missed a lot of childhood experiences. You know, like going to movies, concerts, or other things that kids in their home cultures did.

Interviewer: Do you mean they feel like they missed something as kids?

Dr. Paul: Uh-huh. Some feel that way. And some adult TCKs talk about being angry at their parents for that reason and for making them move away. We also found that some adult TCKs don't really want to get married.

Interviewer: Why's that?

Dr. Paul: Well, some feel that they lost their childhood friends, and they are afraid of losing their husband or wife, too.

Interviewer: What happens to these people?

Dr. Paul: Well, we found that when they start to think about these feelings and talk about them, they become happier and more comfortable with themselves and others.

Interviewer: Very interesting, Dr. Paul. Well, it looks like we are out of time . . .

ANSWER KEY

Build Your Vocabulary *pages 29–30*

B. 1. identity 2. source 3. flexible 4. lifestyle
5. participate 6. comfortable 7. relate to
8. tradition 9. unsure 10. grew up **C. Interact with Vocabulary!** 1. a 2. Most 3. the, the 4. the
5. some 6. the 7. Some 8. the 9. a 10. two

Focus Your Attention *page 31*

A. Signal words: that is, means, or
B. 1. environment = where they live 2. identity = who they are 3. flexible = able to change how they think and act

Listen for Main Ideas *pages 32–33*

B. Topic: up, third culture; Main idea 1: mixture; Main Idea 2: helpful; Main idea 3: problems
C. 1, 3, 4

Listen for Details *page 33*

B. 1. a 2. a 3. b 4. a 5. b 6. a (Note: Item b could also be argued as correct, but the lecturer only speaks explicitly about "relatives," not "school friends.") 7. b 8. a

Talk about the Topic *page 34*

A. 1. Rob 2. Molly 3. Rob **B.** 1. Asking for clarification or confirmation 2. Asking for clarification or confirmation 3. Expressing an opinion 4. Disagreeing

Review Your Notes *page 35*

third culture: . . . that create a third culture; TCK = Third culture kids are children who grow up in a culture different from their parents' native culture.

2 Main ideas	1) Being TCK = helpful	2) Problems of TCKs
Details	- interested in & accept other cultures - learn to be flexible - make **friends quickly** -excellent communication skills	- unsure of **identity** - not comfortable with **relatives** - not have **deep, long-lasting friendships**
Ex. from lecture or own exp.:	**Kids learned Ghanaian culture**	son: "nomad"

Take the Unit Test

1. b 2. b 3. c 4. a and c 5. c 6. c 7. c 8. b
9. b 10. b

Extend the Topic *page 37*

C. Item 2: anger because they missed childhood experiences; don't want to get married/fear of loss

 **TEST** ANTHROPOLOGY: Third Culture Kids

 Listen to each question. Circle the letter of the correct answer.

1. a. by reading about them
   b. by living in them
   c. by sending their children to visit them

2. a. children who grow up in third world countries
   b. children who grow up in a mixture of two or more cultures
   c. children who go to international schools

3. a. American culture
   b. Ghanaian culture
   c. both a and b

4. a. to make friends quickly
   b. to make deep friendships
   c. to accept other cultures

5. a. an interest in other cultures
   b. friends all over the world
   c. fear of other cultures

6. a. They don't like their home culture.
   b. They don't like the host culture.
   c. They are unsure about their identity.

7. a. He likes to move often.
   b. He doesn't like American culture.
   c. He doesn't feel like he belongs in American or Ghanaian culture.

8. a. They don't like people.
   b. They know that they will move again.
   c. They don't believe friends are important.

9. a. nomads
   b. other third culture kids
   c. relatives

10. a. They didn't enjoy being third culture kids.
    b. They liked being third culture kids.
    c. The speaker didn't say.

TEACHING TIPS

UNIT OVERVIEW

In this unit, students will learn about three diets popular today. The lecture focuses on each diet, the Mediterranean Diet, the Best Life Diet, and the Traffic Light Diet, from the perspective of lifestyle change rather than weight loss. Follow-up projects extend the topic to broader issues of fitness and health.

Connect to the Topic *page 38*   *~10 minutes*

Students take a survey about nutrition and diets. Survey questions concern students' food preferences.

Build Your Vocabulary *pages 39–40*   *~15 minutes*

Students study the following words and phrases related to health sciences and diet:

areas (of the world)	involves	nutritious
authorities (in)	is an example of	percent of
comes from	is different from	select
consume	is good for	thinking about
create	is special about	(personal) trainer
feature (of)	journal	was created by
in the world	make wise choices about	

After the Interact with Vocabulary! activity, you may want to have students practice using the boldfaced words with their partners. Knowing collocations can help students expand their vocabularies and increase their fluency.

Focus Your Attention *page 41*   *~10 minutes*

Students learn words and phrases that speakers use to introduce examples:

*For **example**, . . .*
*Chocolate **is a good example of** . . .*
*Our third **example/way is** . . .*

Listen to the Lecture *pages 42–43*   *~30 minutes*

Students discuss a situation about weight gain (Before You Listen) before listening to the unit lecture on diets that promote lifestyle changes. Students then check the main ideas they hear (Listen for Main Ideas). Next they answer multiple-choice items (Listen for Details).
Lecture video time: 5 min. 49 sec.   Number of episodes: 10

Talk about the Topic *page 44* *~20 minutes*

Two students—Hannah and May—discuss the lecture. Part A focuses on matching these students with comments or ideas from the discussion. In Part B, your students work on these discussion strategies:

- Asking for opinions or ideas: "Interesting topic, huh?"
- Asking for clarification or confirmation: "*Which* one?"

For Part C, students are encouraged to use the discussion strategies they've learned. They may use phrases from the student discussion and/or the Discussion Strategy box, or come up with their own. Keep in mind that some students may be reluctant to talk about any unhealthy foods they eat, while others may be very open about discussing them.
Student discussion video time: 1 min. 22 sec.

Review Your Notes *page 45* *~15 minutes*

Students focus on reconstructing their notes, paying particular attention to the examples from the lecture. They are encouraged to compare and complete notes together.

BONUS ACTIVITY

Ask students (or perhaps the most proficient note-takers) to share with the class their strategies for noting examples.

Take the Unit Test *Teacher's Pack page 31* *~15 minutes*

You may want to play the lecture again just before giving the test. Students answer standard test questions about the content of the lecture. Specifically, the test covers the following: what the three diets have in common and features of each diet.

Extend the Topic *page 54* *~30 minutes*
Note that these activities appear at the end of Unit 3b.

- Listening and Discussion: Students listen to and discuss a public service announcement about the link between sleep and weight gain.
- Project/Presentation: Students conduct additional research on the relationship between sleep and diet or sleep and good health, and share their findings with the class.

Focus Your Attention: Try It Out! *page 41*

Speaker: Authorities in the field of nutrition tell us that we need to think about making lifestyle changes if we want to lose some weight. This is different from just "dieting" for a short time. For example, eating more vegetables would be a lifestyle change, for some people. That doesn't mean you can't have a treat now and then! Exercising regularly is another good example of a way to change your lifestyle, if you don't exercise much now. And a third example of a lifestyle change is . . .

Listen for Main Ideas and Listen for Details *pages 42–43*

Health Sciences lecturer: E1 Good morning, everybody. Today, I want to start by having you imagine that you're very hungry. OK? Then I want you to "choose" something to eat. Something you'd buy or fix yourself. So what foods did you select? And why? E2 Well, maybe you were thinking about nutritional value and chose something like a tuna sandwich or a salad. Or, maybe you were thinking "fast and easy" and chose potato chips or a candy bar. Well, let's think for a minute about that "fast and easy" choice. What happens when you eat foods with poor nutritional value—like a candy bar? I can think of two possibilities: One, you won't feel too good after you eat it. And two, you'll add unnecessary body fat. In fact, people in a lot of countries, and particularly the United States, are getting too fat. The CDC, the Center for Disease Control, reports that 23 percent of all Americans are too fat—they're overweight. And although many of them try weight-loss diets, most of them don't succeed. E3 So, today, I want to speak to you about three new, popular diets. Now, what's different about these three diets is that they all involve making wise choices in the foods we consume, and changing how we eat and live every day—not just for a short time. In other words, these diets are about lifestyle. The three diets are the Mediterranean Diet, the Best Life Diet, and the Traffic Light Diet. E4 First is the Mediterranean Diet. This one has been called "the best in the world" by some authorities. Let's examine why. As the name suggests, this diet comes from the Mediterranean area—specifically the Greek island of Crete. Cretans eat a lot of fresh fish, fresh fruit and vegetables, and cheese. And they drink wine, too. E5 Now, the surprising feature of this diet is the amount of olives and olive oil Cretans consume. These are fats and make up about 40 percent of their diet. That sounds like a lot, doesn't it? The thing is—that type of fat is different from the fats in red meats and in other oils. Some even call it a "good fat." Scientific evidence shows that people who follow the Mediterranean Diet are much less likely to develop heart disease than people who eat red meat or other sources of fat. So, not only does the Mediterranean Diet taste great, but it seems to be very good for your heart. And, remember, this diet is about making a lifestyle change—it's not a fast fix to weight or health problems. E6 Well, let's move on to the second diet, the Best Life Diet, created by Oprah Winfrey's personal trainer Bob Greene. This diet claims that it'll help us live the best life possible. It's based on eating a diet filled with lots of grains, fruit and vegetables, foods from milk, and low-calorie/low-fat meats. The Best Life Diet also says that exercise is very important. Makes sense, right? E7 So what's special about this diet? Well, it advises gradual, not immediate, changes in diet and exercise. So, slowly adding in low-fat items while reducing high-fat items is the way to go here. For example, getting rid of snacks like potato chips and soda while adding in fruit and taking more walks. And again, this diet isn't a quick way to lose weight—it's about lifelong changes. E8 Our third diet example is the Traffic Light Diet, by British nutritionist Judith Wills. This one has us think of our food choices like the three colors of a traffic light. Red means stop; yellow means caution—be careful; and green means go. E9 So, if a food is high in fat and calories and not very nutritious, what color would that be? Red, of course. Chocolate cake is a good example of a red food. Now, if the food is a little high in calories but also nutritious, like, say, potatoes, then it's a yellow food. And green foods? Those are the ones low in calories and high in nutrition. Think of things like fruit and vegetables and white fish. These get the green light. Again, as with the other two diets I've discussed today, the idea here is to change how you eat and live every day—to change your lifestyle. E10 Now, between now and next time, I'd like you to keep a food journal. You know, a daily account of all the foods you consume. Then, in class, we'll assess those—and you can see if there are areas where you can make your diet healthier.

Coaching Tips

[1] Note-taking: Using charts How many diets is this lecture going to cover? Three—right! It might be helpful to organize your notes in a chart with three rows. It could look something like this: [see video for note-taking example]. In this example, there's one row for each type of diet. You can write in the name of each diet as you hear it. Then you can add notes about each diet in the column beside the name. Charts are good for note-taking because they organize new information in a clear way.

[2] Critical Thinking: Applying knowledge Have you ever been to the Mediterranean area? What about the island of Crete? Can you find it on a map? Think about where it is from where you are now. Now think about the foods the speaker mentions: fresh fish, vegetables, and fruit. Cheese, olives, and wine. Have you ever had any of these things? Probably so! Thinking about what you already know can help you understand a topic better.

[3] Listening: Identifying examples Speakers often give examples to help you understand an idea. Here, the speaker gives an example of a lifestyle change to help you understand how the Best Life Diet works. How did the speaker signal that an example was coming? She said, "For example," and then gave information about the diet. When you hear the word *example*, be sure to write the information down. Examples are a good way to understand ideas.

[4] Critical Thinking: Responding to a topic You've now heard about three popular diets. What do you think about these diets? Are they all the same? Is one diet better than the others? You might want to write your opinion in the margin—or at the side—of your notes. Thinking about your feelings about things from the lecture can make the lecture information more meaningful.

Talk about the Topic *page 44*

Hannah: Interesting topic, huh? Health and diets.

May: Speaking of diets, you know since I moved here, I've definitely gained weight. And I need to go on a diet!

Hannah: Yeah, I've put on some extra pounds, too.

May: It's the food here!

Hannah: Yeah, I love trying new foods, and there's so much variety here.

May: I know what you mean. For me, I guess I'm just eating some of the wrong things.

Hannah: But, remember, the speaker said we need to make changes in our lifestyle, not just go on a quick diet.

May: You're right. I think I could learn to eat a lot better and then lose weight. You know, I really liked the Traffic Light Diet.

Hannah: *Which* one?

May: The Traffic Light Diet.

Hannah: Ahh.

May: You know, you learn more about which foods are red or yellow or green.

Hannah: Oh, yeah, good idea. So when you make choices, you can think about "going" for it or "stopping"—like, green for "go" and red for "stop"?

May: Exactly! What about you? Are you going to make any changes?

Hannah: Yup, exercise—regular exercise. That'll help me to get fit and drop some pounds. And maybe have more energy.

May: Yeah, that sounds like a good plan.

Hannah: Yeah, I think you need to have a plan; otherwise, you won't make any real changes in your lifestyle.

May: That's true.

Take the Unit Test

1. What does the speaker say about Americans and weight?
2. Which is true of all three diets?
3. What are two features of the Mediterranean Diet? Choose *two* answers.
4. What does the speaker say about olive oil?
5. What might happen to people who eat a lot of red meat?
6. Which diet involves making slow changes in diet and exercise?
7. In the Traffic Light Diet, which color means low in calories and high in nutrition?
8. Which is an example of a "green" food?
9. Which diet is best for losing weight quickly?
10. What do all three diets involve?

Extend the Topic *page 54*

Note that this activity appears at the end of Unit 3b.

Mrs. Daly: Hi, Jessica! I got your message about the mouse—yikes! We'll take care of that. How's our favorite renter doing? You look tired, dear.

Jessica: Mrs. Daly, tired isn't the word for how I feel. I'm way past tired—I'm exhausted! No time for sleep. Also, I've gained a lot of weight.

Mrs. Daly: Well, you know, not enough sleep and weight gain are related. Why aren't you sleeping enough?

Jessica: Oh, you know how it is. Writing papers. Working at the bookstore. Going to parties! There's just not enough time in the day—or night!

Mrs. Daly: Of course you have to do your assignments and go to work. And have a social life! But getting enough rest is really important. Did you know that about 65 percent of Americans don't get enough sleep? And, well, we know that many Americans are, well, let's be honest: a bit too fat!

Jessica: OK, OK. I guess I need to organize my life better so that I can get more sleep. I know I feel a lot better when I have more rest. I know I eat better, too.

Mrs. Daly: I can give you some great tips about time management. Before I was a landlady, I was an event planner.

Jessica: You? No way . . . !

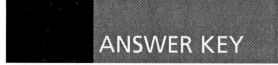

ANSWER KEY

Build Your Vocabulary *pages 39–40*
A. 1. c 2. a 3. c 4. b 5. c 6. b 7. a 8. b 9. c
10. b **B. Interact with Vocabulary!** 1. about
2. of 3. from 4. about 5. in 6. from 7. for
8. about 9. by 10. of

Focus Your Attention *page 41*
A. Signal: For example, is another good example, a third example **B.** 2 (Note: The speaker indicates that there will be at least a third example, but we only hear two.) **C.** eating more vegetables; exercising regularly

Listen for Main Ideas *page 42*
3, 4, 5, 6 (Note: Item 2 is true but isn't a main idea)

Listen for Details *page 43*
B. 1. b 2. a 3. a 4. b 5. b 6. b 7. a 8. b 9. b 10. b

Talk about the Topic *page 44*
A. 1. Hannah, May 2. Hannah, May 3. May
B. 1. Asking for opinions or ideas 2. Asking for clarification or confirmation 3. Asking for clarification or confirmation (Note: Hannah continues by saying, "like green for 'go' and 'red' for stop." She doesn't say "you know." 4. Asking for opinions or ideas

Review Your Notes *page 45*

3 Ex. of new diets	Details of how diet works
1) **Mediterranean**	fresh fish fresh **fruits** & vegetables cheese wine **olives** & olive oil
2) Best Life	grains **fruit** & vegetables foods from **milk** low-calorie, low-fat **meats** diet & exercise
3) **Traffic** Light	red food = **stop** **yellow** food = be careful green **food** = **go**

Take the Unit Test
1. a 2. b 3. a and c 4. c 5. a 6. b 7. a 8. c
9. c 10. a

 **TEST** HEALTH SCIENCES: New Diets

 Listen to each question. Circle the letter of the correct answer.

1. a. Twenty-three percent of Americans are too fat.
   b. Most Americans choose candy for lunch.
   c. Americans usually succeed at weight-loss diets.

2. a. They work in a short time.
   b. They involve lifestyle changes.
   c. They come from the Mediterranean area.

3. a. It includes a lot of olives and olive oil.
   b. It includes a lot of candy and sweets.
   c. It comes from the Greek island of Crete.

4. a. It should not be part of a healthy diet.
   b. It doesn't taste very good.
   c. It is a good fat.

5. a. They might have more heart disease than people who eat good fats.
   b. They might have less heart disease than people who eat good fats.
   c. They won't have any heart disease.

6. a. the Mediterranean Diet
   b. the Best Life Diet
   c. the Traffic Light Diet

7. a. green
   b. yellow
   c. red

8. a. chocolate cake
   b. potatoes
   c. white fish

9. a. the Best Life Diet
   b. the Traffic Light Diet
   c. none of the above

10. a. changing the way we eat and live every day
    b. exercising every day
    c. both a and b

HEALTH SCIENCES
Food Addictions

UNIT OVERVIEW

In this unit, students will look at three food substances that can be addictive when consumed in excess: caffeine, sugar, and chocolate. The lecture focuses on the definition of addiction, foods and drinks that can be addictive, how the three substances affect the body, and why they are not "banned." Follow-up projects extend the topic to broader health issues.

Connect to the Topic *page 46*   *~10 minutes*

Students take a survey about common foods and drink that contain substances that can be addictive. Survey questions ask students which foods and drinks they consume regularly.

Build Your Vocabulary *pages 47–48*   *~15 minutes*

Students study these words and phrases related to foods and addiction:

addictive quality	harmful	period of time
affects	healthy lifestyles	regulates
carries a risk	legal	risk
consequence	(in) moderation	significant amount
crave (something)	natural substance	substances

After the Interact with Vocabulary! activity, you may want to have students practice using the boldfaced words with their partners. Knowing collocations can help students expand their vocabularies and increase their fluency.

Focus Your Attention *page 49*   *~10 minutes*

Students learn how predicting and listening for list signal words can help them take better notes. They try predicting what a lecturer speaking about addictive substances might say, then take notes as they listen. They compare notes with a partner.

Listen to the Lecture *pages 50–51*   *~30 minutes*

Students predict what the lecturer will say, based on images of coffee, chocolate, and sugar (Before You Listen). Students then fill in missing main ideas (Listen for Main Ideas) and complete multiple-choice items (Listen for Details).
Lecture video time: 5 min. 20 sec.   *Number of episodes: 9*

Talk about the Topic   *page 52*   *~20 minutes*

Two students—Michael and Rob—discuss the lecture. Part A focuses on matching these students with comments or ideas from the discussion. Notice that in this unit, your students are identifying who *disagrees* with the statement. In Part B, your students work on these discussion strategies:

- Expressing an opinion: "Sounds like *somebody* has an addiction."
- Disagreeing: "Well, I wouldn't say that."
- Offering a fact or example: "Every Wednesday night there's this live music show on MTV."

For Part C, students are encouraged to use the discussion strategies they've learned. They may use phrases from the student discussion and/or the Discussion Strategy box, or come up with their own. Keep in mind that some students may be reluctant to talk about foods that may be taboo or not widely consumed in their culture, while others may be very open.
Student discussion video time: 1 min. 45 sec.

Review Your Notes   *page 53*   *~15 minutes*

Students focus on reviewing together and then reconstructing their notes, paying attention to supporting details.

BONUS ACTIVITY

You can supplement this activity with a *Jeopardy*-like game where students are given the negative effect of a substance and have to come up with the substance that causes it (for example: feeling low/sugar).

Take the Unit Test   *Teacher's Pack page 37*   *~15 minutes*

You may want to play the lecture again just before giving the test. Students answer standard test questions about the content of the lecture. Specifically, the test covers the following: definition of *addictive*, examples of addictive substances, characteristics of food addictions, and how we can avoid food addictions.

Extend the Topic   *page 55*   *~30 minutes*

- Listening and Discussion: Students listen to a radio ad for a high-energy product and discuss.
- Project/Presentation: Students interview people about consumption patterns and report their findings to the class.

Focus Your Attention:
Try It Out! *page 49*

Speaker: Today, we're discussing addictive substances, and the harmful effects of those substances. Let's take caffeine. What are some harmful effects of caffeine? First, caffeine can make us feel very nervous. Like, we have too much energy. Next, caffeine can cause our bodies to lose water. You know what I'm talking about, right? Never drink coffee before a long road trip! And third, if your body becomes used to caffeine, you may feel tired without it. We've all heard people use the explanation, "Oh, I haven't had my coffee yet . . ."

Listen for Main Ideas and Listen for Details *pages 50–51*

Health Sciences lecturer: **E1** Last time, we looked at diet and healthy lifestyles. Today, we're going to talk about foods and drinks that can be addictive. What does "addictive" mean? Well, it means that a person can't easily stop consuming something. They crave it. In other words, they feel like they need it to feel calm. We usually think of things like drugs or alcohol or cigarettes when we talk about addiction. **E2** But today, we're going to look at three very common substances I bet most of us have consumed. And we'll see how they can be addictive, too, and why that can be harmful. **E3** Let's talk first about caffeine. That's c-a-f-f-e-i-n-e. It's a natural substance that makes people feel excited or more awake. And studies have shown that it's addictive. Can you think of something you drink that contains caffeine? Let's see. There's coffee. And tea. And how about colas, like Pepsi and Coke? These all contain caffeine, and therefore carry the risk of addiction. Does this mean you'll become addicted if you have a coffee now and then? Or a Coke or a cup of tea? No. It's only when you drink several cups or glasses every day that you might experience the addicting quality of these drinks. **E4** So how does caffeine affect our bodies and what are the dangers of a caffeine addiction? Well, too much caffeine can cause your heart to "race." And you may have difficulty sleeping. Caffeine can also cause your body to lose water. And, finally, if you consume a lot of caffeine over a long period of time, and then try to quit it? You might experience headaches. **E5** Here's another example of something common—and addictive. Sugar! You might say "What? There's sugar in all sorts of foods and drinks." You're right. Americans consume an average of 135 pounds of sugar every year—that's 2 to 3 pounds a week! It's pretty hard to get through a day without eating something with sugar in it. Lots of common foods and drinks—like candy, soft drinks, breakfast cereal, even spaghetti sauce—contain sugar! **E6** So what are the dangers of having a sugar addiction? Well, if we eat or drink a lot of it, we might feel "high" or happy at first. But later it can make us feel unhappy or low. And eating a significant amount of sugar can make us fat. Sugar is also bad for our teeth. But, like with caffeine, if we consume a little sugar each day, we probably won't experience addiction. **E7** OK. I've saved the best example for last. At least I think it's the best: chocolate! Here we have sugar, plus a couple of chemicals that are like caffeine. So all of the consequences of caffeine and sugar I mentioned are true for chocolate, too. Which means it could make your heart race, your head hurt, and your teeth bad. It also might make you lose water, feel high but then low, feel restless, and get fat. **E8** But wait a minute! If we know that these substances can be addictive, and that an addiction can harm the body, then why is it socially acceptable to consume these substances? Because, unlike drugs or alcohol, the consumption of caffeine and sugar and chocolate is unregulated. That means there are no laws controlling our consumption. In fact, in many cultures, these three things are considered "luxuries," or very special items that people give as gifts. So, there's this sort of a "double standard" about these substances, right? By that I mean: Because they're legal, it's "OK" to consume them, even though they might cause us harm. **E9** So, if you like caffeine, sugar, and chocolate, what's the answer? Well, it's almost impossible to get through life without consuming these things. From vending machines to movie theaters to your favorite café, they're everywhere you turn. The key is "moderation." This means not too much. Go ahead, enjoy your morning coffee or a piece of chocolate. Just don't overdo it, and you'll be fine!

Coaching Tips

[1] Critical Thinking: Predicting Do you know something about the topic of addiction? Think about what you already know, and then predict what the speaker will talk about in this lecture. Predicting what you might hear is a good way to prepare to hear new information.

[2] Note-taking: Organizing numbered lists How many substances will you be hearing about? Three, right? And which does the speaker say she'll talk about first? Caffeine. So you know that this is the first of three substances. Each substance is a main idea for this lecture. How could you set up your notes? Here's one way to organize your notes when you know you'll be hearing a list of items: [see video for note-taking example].

[3] Listening: Listening for order signals Did you hear the second substance that can be addictive? Were you listening for order words? This time, the speaker says, "Here's another example . . . " You already heard the first example, right? It was caffeine. You could write this example, sugar, as number two. Think ahead: What words might the speaker use to signal the last example?

[4] Critical Thinking: Responding to a topic The speaker talks about the three substances and laws. What does she say about regulation? Think about your culture. Are these substances "luxuries" in your culture? Are they special? Do you think they should be regulated? You could make a note about this in the margin of your notebook. Adding your thoughts to your notes can help you understand a lecture better.

Talk about the Topic *page 52*

Rob: You know what I want right now?

Michael: Don't tell me. Chocolate?

Rob: Yep. I'm totally craving, like, a big piece of chocolate cake with an espresso!

Michael: You don't believe they're bad for you?

Rob: Well, how can chocolate cake and espresso be bad for me when they taste so good?

Michael: Sounds like *somebody* has an addiction. Like you kind of "need" that cake and coffee.

Rob: Well, I wouldn't say that. I mean, I think a craving is different from an addiction.

Michael: Hmm. I don't know if I agree with that. I guess it depends on how badly and how often you crave something.

Rob: Well, that's a good way to put it. Like, I'm craving chocolate and coffee today. But as soon as I have it, I won't really want it again for, I don't know, a few weeks.

Michael: Oh, so then you're not an addict. . . . Tell me what you think about this: Every Wednesday night there's a live music show on MTV. And all I can think about on Wednesdays is getting home to see it. And if for some reason I miss it, I'm really low and depressed!

Rob: Well, for it to be an "addiction," it has to be harmful, right? So, what's the harm in that, do you think?

Michael: Well, I guess I could be studying during that time. But mostly, it just fuels my need to hear good music.

Rob: Well, I think that's a good addiction, in my opinion.

Michael: A good addiction? I like that idea!

Rob: Yeah. You have to have good addictions. It keeps, keeps your head straight . . .

Take the Unit Test

1. What does "addictive" mean?
2. Which three addictive substances does the speaker discuss?
3. Which substance makes people feel more awake?
4. What is one of the dangers of a caffeine addiction?
5. How much sugar do Americans consume each week, on average?
6. What are the dangers of sugar addiction? Choose *two* answers.
7. How does the speaker feel about chocolate?
8. What are some of the dangers of a chocolate addiction?
9. Why is it socially acceptable to consume caffeine, sugar, and chocolate?
10. What can we do to avoid addiction to caffeine, sugar, or chocolate?

Extend the Topic *page 55*

Announcer: Feeling wiped out lately? So tired you just want to sleep all the time? You *have* to try our new breakthrough in delicious, tasty, instant energy. It's . . . Chocojolt!! Now, this isn't just *any* chocolate candy bar. This candy bar was scientifically created to give you that extra boost you need to get through your day. It's not only wonderfully chocolaty, but it's also loaded with an extra punch—caffeine! And lots of it. Need to stay awake during a boring meeting at work? Chocojolt's for you! One bite when you start feeling bored or sleepy, and *wow*! You're wide awake! How about that late night study session? Try Chocojolt! You can't even think about going to sleep, thanks to all that caffeine! We're so sure you'll like new Chocojolt that we have free samples for you. Just e-mail us at chocojolt dot com for your free coupon. Not for children under the age of sixteen because of the addictive qualities of this product.

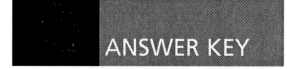

ANSWER KEY

Build Your Vocabulary *pages 47–48*
B. 1. harmful 2. legal 3. consequences 4. crave
5. period of time 6. substances 7. risk
8. regulated 9. moderation 10. affect **C. Interact
with Vocabulary!** 1. healthy 2. natural 3. carries
4. addictive 5. significant

Focus Your Attention *page 49*
B. Caffeine: 1. makes us feel very nervous
2. causes our bodies to lose water 3. feel tired
without it

Listen for Main Ideas *page 50*
B. Topic: Food 1. addictive 2. caffeine, excited
3. sugar 4. Chocolate 5. moderation

Listen for Details *page 51*
B. 1. a 2. b 3. a 4. a 5. a 6. b 7. a 8. a

Talk about the Topic *page 52*
A. 1. Rob 2. Rob 3. Michael 4. Michael, Rob
B. 1. Expressing an opinion 2. Disagreeing
3. Disagreeing 4. Offering a fact or example (Note:
Michael actually says "*a* live music show.")

Review Your Notes *page 53*
I. Dangers of too much **caffeine**: b. difficulty
sleeping c. body loses **water** d. **Try to quit?**
headaches; II. Dangers of too much **sugar**: a. feel
high and then **low** c. bad for **teeth**; III. Dangers of
too much **chocolate**: a. **heart** races b. **difficulty**
sleeping c. **body** loses **water** e. feel **high** and
then **low** f. **bad** for **teeth** g. get **fat**; The key =
moderation

Take the Unit Test
1. c 2. a 3. a 4. a 5. b 6. a and c 7. a 8. b
9. b 10. a

Extend the Topic *page 55*
C. 1. Chocojolt; loaded with caffeine, gives energy

UNIT 3b TEST HEALTH SCIENCES: Food Addictions

Listen to each question. Circle the letter of the correct answer.

1. a. not letting us easily stop consuming something
   b. causing us to crave something and need it to feel calm
   c. both a and b

2. a. caffeine, sugar, and chocolate
   b. milk, sugar, and chocolate
   c. caffeine, sugar, and bread

3. a. coffee
   b. sugary foods
   c. both a and b

4. a. The body loses water.
   b. You feel low.
   c. neither a nor b

5. a. 135 pounds
   b. 2 to 3 pounds
   c. The speaker doesn't say.

6. a. It can make us fat.
   b. It keeps us awake.
   c. It can make us feel high and then low.

7. a. She likes chocolate.
   b. She thinks chocolate is very bad.
   c. She doesn't say.

8. a. It can make us feel calm and make our teeth bad.
   b. It can give us headaches and cause weight gain.
   c. It can cause weight gain and make us sleep too much.

9. a. are luxuries
   b. are not regulated by laws
   c. because they are illegal substances

10. a. enjoy them in moderation
    b. never eat or drink them
    c. overdo it with them

TEACHING TIPS

UNIT OVERVIEW

In this unit, students will learn about an important concept in global business: the challenge of communicating effectively across cultures. The lecture focuses on two styles of communication, high context and low context, and examines communication skills and strategies for communicating effectively with both styles. Follow-up projects extend the topic to gender differences in communication styles.

Connect to the Topic *page 56*   *~10 minutes*

The opening image is a high-context advertisement showing a man with a milk mustache and a headline that reads "Mind by Masi." Masi Oka is a Japanese American actor who has played the role of a superhero who can change the future. You may want to have students familiar with the actor explain the ad. Below is a survey about communication styles. Survey questions prompt students to evaluate their preferred speaking and listening styles.

Build Your Vocabulary *pages 57–58*   *~15 minutes*

Students study these words and phrases related to business communication:

appealed	nonverbal	project
appeal to	communication	recognize
become partners	occurred	recognize ideas
(share) comments	partners	sends a clear
complete a project	problems occur	message
made a comment	when	transfer (skills)
message	productive	transferred to
nonverbal		

Focus Your Attention *page 59*   *~10 minutes*

Students learn cues that speakers use when comparing and contrasting ideas:

Signal words and phrases: **Stating key words:**
On the other hand, . . .   *loudly*
However, . . .   *slowly*
That said, . . .

Listen to the Lecture *pages 60–61*   *~30 minutes*

Students discuss the pictures showing businesspeople interacting (Before You Listen) before listening to the unit lecture on low- and high-context styles of communication. Students then select items from a word bank to complete an outline of main ideas (Listen for Main Ideas). Next they identify true/false statements and correct the false statements (Listen for Details). You may want to instruct students to write the corrected false statements at the bottom of the page.
Lecture video time: 6 min. 8 sec.   Number of episodes: 11

> **NOTE**
>
> Remember that with the DVD, you can play the lecture in different modes: video, video with Presentation Points, video with Coaching Tips, video with subtitles, video with subtitles and Coaching Tips, and video with Coaching Tips and Presentation Points. (We do not recommend playing the video with both the Presentation Points and subtitles on.) You can also play the lecture as audio only, using the CD.

Talk about the Topic   *page 62*   *~20 minutes*

Two students—Molly and Hannah—discuss the lecture. Part A focuses on matching these students with comments or ideas from the discussion. In Part B, your students work on these discussion strategies:

- Expressing an opinion: "The two concepts are interesting."
- Offering a fact or example: "Well, I used to work with this American woman . . . "

For Part C, students are encouraged to use the discussion strategies they've learned. They may use phrases from the student discussion and/or the Discussion Strategy box, or come up with their own. Keep in mind that some students may be reluctant to discuss personal experiences involving difficulties in communicating with individuals from other cultures.
Student discussion video time: 1 min. 37 sec.

Review Your Notes   *page 63*   *~15 minutes*

Students focus on reconstructing their notes, paying attention to key words and phrases, and contrasting details.

> **BONUS ACTIVITY**
>
> Explore the differences in nonverbal communication styles in your classroom. Working in pairs, students can observe gestures and facial expressions used by speakers from different cultures or age groups, and report their findings to the class.

Take the Unit Test   *Teacher's Pack page 43*   *~15 minutes*

You may want to play the lecture again just before giving the test. Students answer standard test questions about the content of the lecture. Specifically, the test covers the following: definition of *context*; characteristics of high-context communicators; characteristics of low-context communicators; and preferences of high- and low-context communicators.

Extend the Topic   *page 72*   *~30 minutes*
Note that these activities appear at the end of Unit 4b.

- Listening and Discussion: Students listen to a researcher talk about the differences between male and female communication styles, then discuss.
- Project/Presentation: The unit concludes with a role play highlighting communication differences between men and women.

Focus Your Attention:
Try It Out! *page 59*

Speaker: Let's look at two different styles of communication. With the first style, people use *words* to communicate their ideas. For them, *telling* is the best way to communicate. With the second style, people use their *bodies* to communicate their ideas. For these people, *showing* is the best way to communicate. So as you can see, these two styles . . .

Listen for Main Ideas and Listen for Details *pages 60–61*

Business lecturer: **E1** Today I want to talk about something that everyone who works in international business must learn to do: Communicate across cultures. International businesspeople come from all different cultures, right? So they have different ways of communicating—both in how they express their ideas, and how they receive their ideas. **E2** Now, just to be clear, I'm not talking about the use of a particular language—English or French or Chinese or whatever. I'm talking about communication style within a language. Communication style means how we exchange information, how we show our feelings, and how we understand other people. **E3** So, as international businesspeople, how do we "communicate across cultures"? Well, first, by understanding the communication styles we and others use, and second, by transferring that knowledge to the workplace. **E4** So let's get started. Now, what communication styles do people use? Well, basically, there are two. One is "low context" and the other is "high context." That's low-context communication style and high-context communication style. **E5** Let's first define "context." Well, context is the situation or surrounding information—the nonverbal information—that helps a person understand a message better. For example, someone walking in the door right now would understand that we're having a class just by seeing the context here, right? Desks, students taking notes, me standing here talking to you, etcetera. That's context. **E6** So, turning to our first communication style. Low-context communication is when a person expresses an idea directly. They put the important information into words. In low-context communication, we don't need the context—or nonverbal information—to communicate. The context is low. Words are what's important. Who uses low-context communication? Well, culturally speaking, most North Americans and Europeans do. Let's look at an example. Say we have an advertising agency, and two professionals—both Americans—are discussing an idea for an ad for athletic shoes. One says, "I think the ad should feature World Cup players." The other says, "Oh no. I disagree. I think the ad should show everyday people." See how each expressed their ideas very directly, with just words? This is how low-context communicators operate. **E7** Now, let's look at high-context communication. High-context communication occurs when a person expresses an idea indirectly, through body movement, facial expressions, even silence. They show the important information, nonverbally, rather than speaking it. The context is very significant to the meaning of the message. The context is high. Generally speaking, this style of communication is typical of Asians, Africans, and Middle Easterners. An example might be two Egyptian bankers creating a loan plan for a local business. The first banker shows his partner a plan he put together the night before: numbers and dates and so on. The partner reads the plan, and responds by remaining silent. The first banker gets the message—his partner doesn't like it. He "said" so with his silence! **E8** Now, it's important to recognize that each of these two communication styles has its strengths and its weaknesses. Low-context communicators are often very productive because they quickly and clearly identify business problems and find short-term solutions. And they're fast at developing projects. But, because of this fast style, they may not build strong, long-term business relationships. So, if you're working with low-context communicators, you need to remember this: Important ideas and feelings are often expressed very directly and forcefully. **E9** Now, high-context communicators, on the other hand, may seem to be slow. They often don't move quickly to find solutions because they want to get more information and opinions first—they don't want to make mistakes. Also, they're careful with their opinions because they want to preserve their relationships with other people. So if you're working with high-context communicators, remember this: Things may happen more slowly, and important messages are often sent nonverbally. **E10** So let's now combine our two earlier examples. Let's say our Egyptian banker contacts the American at the ad agency. He tells her his bank would like to do some advertising. So, the American creates two ads: One shows the bank's name in huge, bright letters. Then it lists all the bank's services and several comments from satisfied customers. The other ad shows only a picture of a woman smiling in front of her bakery, with the words "Business loans for everyone" and the bank's name at the bottom of the ad. Can you guess which ad the Egyptian banker liked best, and why? The one with the picture of a happy woman and her bakery, of course. The high-context ad appealed to the person with the high-context communication style. And even though the ad agency representative was from a low-context culture, she understood that her customer was from a high-context culture. E11 OK? Well, that's all for now. For next time, I want you to think about which kind of communicator you are—high- or low-context. And what experiences you've had "communicating across cultures."

Coaching Tips

[1] Note-taking: Using abbreviations The speaker uses the phrase "communication styles" a lot. Have you noticed this? Instead of writing out both words in your notes every time, you could use an abbreviation. Maybe *c.s.*, for example. It's a good idea to write the phrase out the first time, with the abbreviation beside it. Then you can use just the abbreviation the rest of the time. Using abbreviations can be fun—and fast!

[2] Note-taking: Noting comparisons You're about to begin noting some details about low-context communication. Do you remember what the other style is called? High-context. Right. From their names, you can guess that they are different. You can also guess that the speaker will be making comparisons between the two styles. One way to note comparisons is with a chart. When you review your notes, a chart can help you quickly see how things are alike and different. Here's how your chart, comparing the two styles, might look: [see video for note-taking example].

[3] Note-taking and Listening: Contrast What does the speaker mean when he says "High-context communicators on the other hand . . . "? The phrase "on the other hand" shows that the speaker is going to contrast or clearly show the differences between low- and high-context communicators. Here's how your notes may look now: [see video for note-taking example].

[4] Critical Thinking: Inferencing What's your guess? What kind of ad do you think the Egyptian banker will want? You know that he uses a high-context style of communication. That is, he prefers to get information from the situation, not from words. Think about which ad is high context, and which is low context. With this information, you can use inference to decide which ad the banker chooses. Listen on and see if you're right!

Talk about the Topic *page 62*

Hannah: So, what did you think of the lecture—all of that high- and low-context stuff?

Molly: Well, the two concepts are interesting—I mean for a general understanding of communication differences across cultures.

Hannah: Right, I agree. The lecture helped me understand communication better. Like, I know it's a generalization to say, for example, that Americans are low-context communicators and Koreans are high-context communicators, but it's basically true, in my experience.

Molly: Oh really? What's been your experience?

Hannah: Well, I used to work with this American woman, in the same office, and she said everything very directly, like "this is terrible" or "this is super" or "I hate that" or "I love this."

Molly: Hmm. And you wouldn't do that in Korea?

Hannah: No, normally, you'd be indirect. You wouldn't say things so directly. I guess we're more of a high-context culture. We kind of wait for people to reach an agreement; we don't want to announce our personal feelings so much.

Molly: So then you didn't get along with this American woman?

Hannah: Well, at first, no. But then I figured out that that was just her communication style. She just said everything very directly—and then I didn't take it so personally. I realized it was just a cultural thing.

Molly: That's a good thing to understand.

Hannah: Yeah, it was good for me to figure that out, actually.

Molly: Good, then you don't get offended by anything.

Take the Unit Test

1. What is the main idea of the lecture?
2. To communicate across cultures, what must international businesspeople do? Choose *two* answers.
3. What does "context" mean?
4. Which is most important to a low-context communicator?
5. What does the athletic shoe ad example show?
6. Which is an example of a culture with low-context communication?
7. Which one is *not* true about low-context communicators?
8. How do high-context communicators express themselves? Choose *two* answers.
9. Why does the Egyptian banker choose the ad with the happy woman and her bakery?
10. Which style of communication does the speaker say is better?

Extend the Topic *page 72*

Note that this activity appears at the end of Unit 4b.

Host: Dr. Elizabeth Cameron, welcome to our show.

Dr. Cameron: It's great to be here.

Host: I think the question that many people want to know is, do men and women communicate differently?

Dr. Cameron: Well, in Western cultures, the short answer is yes.

Host: Really? In what ways?

Dr. Cameron: Well, some people who study communication say that men and women talk like they come from different planets. You know, like "men are from Mars, and women are from Venus."

Host: Ah, yes. We've all heard that expression.

Dr. Cameron: But other people, like me, think that they're not so different. Maybe more like men and women come from different regions—say, Northern California and Southern California.

Host: Hmm. Could you explain that more?

Dr. Cameron: Sure. My studies show that women like to form relationships with people as they talk to them. Women try to make a connection with the other person, usually by sharing their feelings and experiences. They want the other person, or other people listening, to feel like joining in the conversation.

Host: And we men don't do this, huh?

Dr. Cameron: Well, sometimes. But most often men clearly say just what they're thinking. They usually just want to give information to show that they're knowledgeable. They also often see a conversation as a chance to show their power. They may say something like "You think *you're* busy, well, let me tell you just how busy I am."

Host: And what might a woman say in this situation?

Dr. Cameron: Oh, she might say something like, "Oh, you *sound* like I *feel*: really tired. Did you have a super busy week, too?"

Host: Interesting! So, are there other differences in how men and women communicate? For example, do they express *opinions* differently?

Dr. Cameron: Well, that's an interesting question . . .

ANSWER KEY

Build Your Vocabulary *pages 57–58*

B. 1. message 2. partner 3. occur 4. appeal 5. nonverbal 6. project 7. recognize 8. comments 9. productive 10. transfer **C. Interact with Vocabulary!** 1. partners in an Internet business 2. transferred to our other office in Hong Kong 3. nonverbal communication rather than 4. to complete this project 5. sends a clear message 6. details appeal to Americans 7. made a comment about 8. to recognize workers' ideas 9. occur when businesspeople don't

Focus Your Attention *page 59*

A. Two different styles of communication **B.** 1st **style**: words, telling; 2nd **style**: bodies, showing

Before You Listen

This activity is meant to introduce the students to the topic of business communication. They may notice things like eye contact, personal space, facial expressions, and formality of attire.

Listen for Main Ideas *page 60*

B. Topic: Working, communication styles; Main idea 1: context; Main idea 2: high

Listen for Details *page 61*

B. 1. T 2. F (two) 3. F (nonverbal) 4. F (does) 5. F (words) 6. T 7. T 8. F (high-) 9. F (slowly) 10. T

Talk about the Topic *page 62*

A. 1. Molly 2. Hannah 3. Hannah
B. 1. Expressing an opinion 2. Expressing an opinion, Offering a fact or example 3. Offering a fact or example 4. Expressing an opinion

Review Your Notes *page 63*

2nd column: no; directly; in words; develop projects quickly; long-term relationships; 3rd column: Egyptian banker chooses picture of woman and bakery; Africans, Asians, Middle Easterners; get information and opinions first; relationships; slow

Take the Unit Test

1. b 2. a and c 3. b 4. b 5. c 6. c 7. b 8. b and c 9. a 10. a

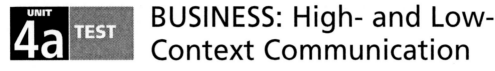

BUSINESS: High- and Low-Context Communication

Listen to each question. Circle the letter of the correct answer.

1. a. to tell businesspeople to visit other cultures
    b. to help businesspeople communicate better
    c. to teach businesspeople another language

2. a. learn about communication styles
    b. change their communication styles
    c. use what they know about communication styles in the workplace

3. a. the words a person uses
    b. a situation or surrounding information
    c. the way a person talks

4. a. the situation
    b. words
    c. work

5. a. how World Cup players communicate
    b. how high-context communicators operate
    c. how low-context communicators operate

6. a. African culture
    b. Asian culture
    c. European culture

7. a. They solve business problems quickly.
    b. They make long-term business relationships.
    c. They finish projects on time.

8. a. They talk quickly.
    b. They ask people for their opinions.
    c. They send messages nonverbally.

9. a. because its high-context message appeals to him
    b. because its low-context message appeals to him
    c. because he likes the ad agency

10. a. He says they both have strengths and weaknesses.
    b. He says high-context communication is better.
    c. He says low-context communication is better.

TEACHING TIPS

UNIT OVERVIEW

In this unit, students will learn about different concepts related to planning and leading international business meetings. The lecture focuses on three aspects of meeting management: time, people, and resources such as technology. Follow-up projects extend the topic to group dynamics.

Connect to the Topic   *page 64*   *~10 minutes*

Students reflect on their experience attending or organizing events by completing a checklist and discussing results in pairs.

Build Your Vocabulary   *pages 65–66*   *~15 minutes*

Students study these words and phrases related to business meeting leadership:

approach	customers	one of many variables
challenge	know your customer	resources
the challenge of	manage	responsibility
concept	manage time	took the right
concept in business	maximize	approach to
conclude	maximized their time	valuable resource
concluded by	my responsibility as	variables

Focus Your Attention   *page 67*   *~10 minutes*

Students learn phrases that lecturers use to signal main idea summaries:

The bottom line about time is . . .   *In short, we can say . . .*
The central point is that time is . . .   *In conclusion, it's clear that . . .*
Let me conclude by saying . . .   *What this all means is . . .*

Students also practice note-taking with these symbols:

→	results in	≠	opposite or doesn't mean
↑	increases or goes up	&	and
↓	decreases or goes down	#	number
=	means or is the same as	$	money or dollars

For the Interact with Vocabulary! activity, you may want to encourage students to first notice the boldfaced words and explain that the boldfaced words form collocations when paired correctly.

Listen to the Lecture   *pages 68–69*   *~30 minutes*

Students consider questions about a meeting scenario (Before You Listen) before listening to the unit lecture on effectively managing international business meetings. Students then draw from a word bank to complete an outline of the main ideas (Listen for Main Ideas). Next they identify true/false statements and correct the false statements (Listen for Details).
Lecture video time: 6 min. 10 sec.   Number of episodes: 9

NOTE

Remember that with the DVD, you can play the lecture in different modes: video, video with Presentation Points, video with Coaching Tips, video with subtitles, video with subtitles and Coaching Tips, and video with Coaching Tips and Presentation Points. (We do not recommend playing the video with both the Presentation Points and subtitles on.) You can also play the lecture as audio only, using the CD.

Talk about the Topic *page 70*   *~20 minutes*

Two students—Rob and May—discuss the lecture. Part A focuses on matching these students with comments from the discussion. In Part B, your students work on these discussion strategies:

- Expressing an opinion: "Yeah, so I guess that shows good people management skills."
- Agreeing: "Well, that's true."
- Offering a fact or example: "Let's take our class, as an example. So, there's the challenge of time . . . "

For Part C, students are encouraged to use the discussion strategies they've learned. They may use phrases from the student discussion or come up with their own. Keep in mind that some students may have little or no experience with meetings while others may have extensive experience.
Student discussion video time: 1 min. 48 sec.

Review Your Notes *page 71*   *~15 minutes*

Students focus on reconstructing their notes, paying attention to main ideas and key details as well as examples.

BONUS ACTIVITY

Have students plan an event (for example, a class awards ceremony, neighborhood party, or school reunion). Working in small groups, students can create a chart detailing organizing challenges and defining strategies for managing the time, people, and resources involved.

Take the Unit Test *Teacher's Pack page 49*   *~15 minutes*

You may want to play the lecture again just before giving the test. Students answer standard test questions about the content of the lecture. Specifically, the test covers the following: the challenges of managing people, managing time, and managing resources.

Extend the Topic *page 73*   *~30 minutes*

- Listening and Discussion: Students listen to a coach describe different kinds of individuals and how they affect group dynamics. Then they discuss in small groups.
- Project/Presentation: Students role-play a scenario demonstrating group dynamics.

AUDIOSCRIPT

Focus Your Attention: Try It Out! *page 67*

Speaker: Now, let's talk about media systems. A well-planned media system results in a better meeting. Of course, you must have an LCD projector and a computer with business software. But also think about the microphone and speakers. Remember, when listeners can't hear clearly, their interest goes down fast, and the time that is wasted goes up. As we know, wasting time is the opposite of making money. So the central point here is good media means better meetings. OK, so let's move on to talking . . .

Listen for Main Ideas and Listen for Details *pages 68–69*

Business lecturer: E1 How many of you have ever organized a group of people—say, like a study group or an English club, or even a party? Not easy, right? Lots of variables, huh? Well, today we're going to examine the three main challenges of leading an international business meeting. And they are one, managing time; two, managing people; and three, managing resources. E2 Let's start with the most basic one: time. In business, there's the expression "Time is money." Has everyone heard that before— "Time is money"? Well, we can apply this idea to our discussion about business meetings. Every minute spent in a meeting needs to be used well. As the American carmaker Henry Ford said, "It has been my observation that most people get ahead during the time that others waste." He means time is valuable. If we want to make progress, we have to use it well. E3 As the meeting manager, you can manage time by following one simple rule: Create an agenda, and stick to it. It sounds easy, huh? Well, no—when working with an international mix of people, this isn't easy. Americans, for example, are known for being prompt. Other cultures—Southern Europeans and Latin Americans, for example—have a less formal approach to time. It's your responsibility as meeting manager to make the rules. For example, if someone is talking on and on and on, you've got to bring the group back to the agenda. I call this "staying on task." By managing the clock throughout the meeting, you'll show everyone that you respect their time. E4 OK, next let's look at the people aspect of running an international meeting. Does everyone remember the concepts of high- and low-context communication? Good. Well, as a meeting manager, it's very important that you recognize who among the meeting participants are high-context communicators, and who are low-context communicators. Why? Because on the one hand, you're going to have some members, say, your North American businesspeople, wanting to get straight to work the minute the meeting starts. Their laptops, or whatever, are out. And they're ready to talk business! On the other hand, other members, say, your South American and Vietnamese or Thai businesspeople, may want to spend a little time getting to know each other first. You know, sipping their coffee and chitchatting, and making small talk. Both approaches are fine. It's up to you to manage these differences. E5 How? Well, let's look for the answer in another challenge of managing people. This challenge relates to managing dynamics—that's d-y-n-a-m-i-c-s. This is the energy created when people interact. We can start with seating. You want to arrange the room in a way that maximizes the energy, maximizes discussion. This may mean you divide friends, and put strangers together. Round tables are good for improving eye contact, and for discussion. However, be careful how many people you put in an area; different cultures like different amounts of personal space. For example, most Americans like about 18 inches of space around them. Any closer, and they're likely to move back, away from the group. Not productive. E6 So, returning to our high-/low-context example, can you see a solution? Maybe you seat your participants around the table—with plenty of space—mixing the high- and low-context communicators. And mixing the personalities to balance the group energy. The bottom line about managing people is, you've got to first understand the cultural differences. As they say in the business world: Know your customer! Then, balance those dynamics. Last note on this one: If you want to take it a step further, educate your participants at the very start of the meeting with a quick "ice-breaker"—a warm-up activity—that reminds everyone to respect each other's cultures. E7 All right. Our last challenge is managing meeting resources. Gee, how many of us have been in a meeting where the presenter's microphone sounds like a 1930s radio broadcast, right? Or the projector is so far from the screen that you can barely read the slides? It's your responsibility to provide the resources—and support—that will make the meeting successful. Like what? Well, you should have an LCD projector and a laptop with all the usual business software. You'll also need a microphone and a media system that works. And don't forget the value of an old-fashioned flipchart, or dry-erase board, and markers. E8 And if you're organizing a "virtual" meeting, you'll need teleconferencing or videoconferencing technology. And finally—super important note here—test out everything yourself before the meeting to be sure everything is "a go." Now remember that some participants may not have used newer technologies before. And that's where the support comes in. You need a "techie" who can fix anything that goes wrong. Never be afraid to ask for help. **E9** Let me conclude with this: Meet the challenges of managing time, people, and technology, and you'll be rewarded with a successful international business meeting. And success, as they say in business, is the bottom line!

Coaching Tips

[1] Listening: Identifying topics through questions
The speaker begins by asking several questions. Why do you think he does this? Speakers often use questions to get the listeners' attention—to get them interested in the topic. As the listener, you can get a good idea of what the lecture is going to be about, based on these questions. Think about your answers to the questions. This will help you get ready to hear and understand the new information as the speaker gives it.

[2] Note-taking: Using abbreviations The speaker repeats this expression twice. This means the idea is important. Can you think of a way to write this idea using symbols? Here the word *is* between two things tells you that the two things are equal. You can show the idea by using the equal sign. You can use the dollar sign for money. Here's one way to note this: [see video for note-taking example]. By using symbols, you can quickly write information in your notes.

[3] Critical Thinking: Using your imagination
Imagine a room full of international business people, seated at round tables. How's "your meeting" going? Is there eye contact? Who needs more personal space? When you use your imagination to process information you've heard, that information can become more meaningful.

[4] Listening: Identifying summaries The speaker signals a summary of this part of his lecture with a business expression—did you hear it? He says, "The bottom line. . . " Another way to signal that a point is finished is to say "Finally," or "Let me conclude with this." As you listen to the rest of the lecture, see if you can hear these expressions.

Talk about the Topic   *page 70*

Rob: What did you think about today's talk?

May: I thought it was interesting, just not practical for me. I don't think I'm ever going to go into international business.

Rob: Well, no matter what, you'll probably have to organize a meeting at some point in your life.

May: You think? I'm considering teaching, actually.

Rob: That's great. Well, let's take our class, as an example. So, there's the challenge of time: Our

instructor has to manage the clock by making sure that the class starts on time.

May: Well, that's true.

Rob: And then he also has to make sure that some students don't keep talking through the whole class.

May: Thankfully! And I guess he creates an "agenda" for each class which we follow.

Rob: Yeah. So, those are all time management skills. What about people management? He has us do the group work—that's a good example. You know? And there's always a lot of cultural diversity in the room.

May: Yeah, that's a good one. I like how he mixes the students—the dynamics of my group have always been good.

Rob: Mine too, I agree.

May: Yeah, so I guess that shows good people management skills.

Rob: Yeah. What about the third challenge of organizing a meeting: managing the resources?

May: Well, there's the dry-erase board.

Rob: And the markers that he loses every day!

May: Or the LCD projector that he can never shut down?

Rob: And he has to get someone in the front row to help him?

May: Oh!

Rob: Every day!

May: So, I guess managing resources is a skill that our instructor needs to improve on.

Rob: Well—two out of three isn't bad.

Take the Unit Test

1. What is the main idea of the lecture?
2. Which meeting challenges does the lecturer discuss?
3. How should time be managed in meetings?
4. What does "staying on task" mean?
5. Why does the speaker discuss high-context and low-context communicators?
6. What are "dynamics"?
7. What should a meeting manager do? Choose *two* answers.
8. What should a meeting manager *not* do?
9. Which resources does the speaker suggest a meeting manager use?
10. How can a "techie" help a meeting manager?

Extend the Topic *page 73*

Reporter: Coach, coach, you just won the biggest game of the year! No one thought you could win today. How did you do it?

Coach: Well, it wasn't me—it was our team. We have great dynamics.

Reporter: Dynamics? Can you tell our viewers what you mean?

Coach: We have the right mix of people. For example, every team needs an agitator.

Reporter: An agitator?

Coach: You know, someone who questions everything—the player who makes the team think about change. And of course, you need a leader—someone who sees where the team needs to go next.

Reporter: Right!

Coach: Oh, and you need to have the glue as well.

Reporter: The glue?

Coach: Yeah, you know, the person who brings everybody together and works out the problems. And this season we definitely had a bunch of workhorses!

Reporter: Horses?

Coach: *Work*horses. Hard workers. Anyway, basically, you just have to be ready. When the horn sounds, everybody has to be ready to play—to do their part. That's the bottom line.

Reporter: OK, thanks, coach! There you have it, the keys to a winning team!

ANSWER KEY

Build Your Vocabulary *pages 65–66*

B. 1. b 2. a 3. a 4. b 5. c 6. a 7. b 8. a 9. b
10. a **C. Interact with Vocabulary!** 1. e 2. c 3. a
4. b 5. d 6. i 7. j 8. h 9. g 10. f

Focus Your Attention *page 67*

A. the central point here is **B.** results in →, and &, and &, goes down ↓, and &, goes up ↑, opposite of ≠, money $, means =

Listen for Main Ideas *page 68*

B. Topic: challenges, managing, international
1. time 2. people 3. resources

Listen for Details *page 69*

B. 1. F (Time is money) 2. T 3. F (more)
4. F (The meeting manager) 5. F (Not all) 6. T
7. F (a mix of communicators) 8. F (Americans)
9. F (whatever resources are needed) 10. F (should check himself/herself)

Talk about the Topic *page 70*

A. 1. May (Note: May actually says, "I'm considering teaching, actually.") 2. Rob 3. Rob;
B. 1. Offering a fact or example 2. Agreeing
3. Expressing an opinion (Note: May actually says, " . . . so *I guess* that shows . . . " 4. Offering a fact or example 5. Expressing an opinion

Review Your Notes *page 71*

international business meeting 1) a. money
b. agenda c. on task 2) people, low-context communicators a. created when people interact b. strangers, personal, 18"; cult difs + dynamics 3) a2) laptop, a3) microphone a5) markers b. everything c. fix anything wrong

Take the Unit Test

1. b 2. c 3. a 4. c 5. a 6. b 7. b and c 8. c
9. a 10. c

BUSINESS: Managing International Meetings

Listen to each question. Circle the letter of the correct answer.

1. a. to help businesspeople save time
   b. to help businesspeople have better meetings
   c. to help businesspeople make more money

2. a. time, money, resources
   b. money, people, time
   c. time, people, resources

3. a. by following an agenda
   b. by being prompt
   c. by being less formal about time

4. a. starting to work quickly
   b. making meeting rules
   c. following the agenda

5. a. because they work differently
   b. because they disagree in meetings
   c. because they like to get to know each other

6. a. long discussions in meetings
   b. the energy made by people working together
   c. reports that tell what happened in a meeting

7. a. learn everyone's name
   b. balance the group dynamics
   c. understand people's cultural differences

8. a. put strangers together
   b. use round tables
   c. have people sit very close to each other

9. a. an LCD projector, a laptop, and a media system
   b. a laptop, a video camera, and a microphone
   c. markers, a microphone, and a TV

10. a. by helping set up the room
    b. by keeping the meeting on time
    c. by fixing anything that goes wrong

TEACHING TIPS

UNIT OVERVIEW

In this unit, students will hear about concepts related to financial management. The lecture focuses on five tips (and supporting examples) for financial security. Follow-up projects extend the topic to money idioms.

Connect to the Topic *page 74*   *~10 minutes*

Students take a survey about finances. Survey questions concern students' plans for the future and how they handle money.

Build Your Vocabulary *pages 75–76*   *~15 minutes*

Students study these words and phrases related to finances and security:

annual (income)	establish (a savings	prepare for
be careful with	account)	emergencies
be pleased at	the first step toward	providing for (your
credit cards	gave tips	family)
debt	go into debt	required
deposit (money)	hopes and dreams	statistics
earn	(pay) interest	time and money
earns money	investment	

For the Interact with Vocabulary! activity, you may want to encourage students to first notice the boldfaced words. Figuring out these collocations can help students more quickly unscramble the sentences.

Focus Your Attention *page 77*   *~10 minutes*

Students learn to listen for imperative verbs introducing advice:

Get a college degree.
Put some money in the bank each month.
Try not to use credit cards. OR Don't use credit cards.

Listen to the Lecture *pages 78–79*   *~30 minutes*

Based on the photo, students imagine what financial advice the father is giving his daughter (Before You Listen). Students next listen to the unit lecture on financial planning, then identify the five strategies from the lecture (Listen for Main Ideas) and answer multiple-choice questions (Listen for Details).
Lecture video time: 6 min. 41 sec.   *Number of episodes: 8*

Talk about the Topic *page 80*   *~20 minutes*

Two students—Michael and Hannah—discuss the lecture. Part A focuses on matching these students with comments or ideas from the discussion. In Part B, your students work on these discussion strategies:

- Asking for opinions or ideas: "How financially secure would you say *you* are?"
- Asking for clarification or confirmation: "I'm a little confused—why are you studying economics, then?"

For Part C, students are encouraged to use the discussion strategies they've learned. They may use phrases from the student discussion or come up with their own. Keep in mind that some students may be reluctant to talk about their finances, while others may be very open. *Student discussion video time: 1 min. 47 sec.*

Review Your Notes *page 81*   *~15 minutes*

Students focus on reconstructing their notes, paying attention to key words and details.

BONUS ACTIVITY

Have students work with a formula for determining interest on credit cards or interest on savings. They can also figure out what completing their current degree program will cost (in cases where students do not pay tuition and other costs, you can have them research the cost of education at another institution or in another country).

Take the Unit Test *Teacher's Pack page 55*   *~15 minutes*

You may want to play the lecture again just before giving the test. Students answer standard test questions about the content of the lecture. Specifically, the test covers the following: why we need to think about financial security, tips offered by the speaker, and details about each tip.

Extend the Topic *page 90*   *~30 minutes*
Note that these activities appear at the end of Unit 5b.

- Listening and Discussion: Students listen to contestants on a game show compete based on their knowledge of money idioms. Students then discuss.
- Project/Presentation: Students role-play a scene involving money idioms.

Focus Your Attention: Try It Out! *page 77*

Speaker: Now, some of you may have heard these ideas from your parents. But it never hurts to hear it again. My first piece of advice is this: Finish your studies. Whether you're in high school or in college, this is extremely important. If you don't, it'll be much harder to go back to school when you're older. Second: Save some money for emergencies. We all have emergencies now and then, right? If you put some money into a special account, you'll have an emergency fund. You won't have to worry about how to pay for a car repair, for example. Final tip: Don't use credit cards if you don't have to. If you *want* but don't *need* something, I say pay with real money.

Listen for Main Ideas and Listen for Details *pages 78–79*

Economics lecturer: E1 Today's talk is very important for your future. In fact, it may be one of the most important talks you'll ever hear about your finances and your financial future. E2 I'm going to present five strategies—or tips—that will help you have a strong financial future. Think for a moment about some of your hopes and dreams. Maybe you want to travel to exotic places, see the world. Perhaps you plan on buying a house. Are you married or are you planning to get married and have a family? You may be thinking about having a secure, comfortable lifestyle and providing well for your children. So, what do all those things require? Money, of course! Then, let's get to those five financial strategies so you can have enough money for your hopes and dreams to come true. E3 Number one: Get a college degree, even if you think you don't need one. Completing a college degree is usually the first step toward financial security. It's a big investment, certainly. Lots of time and money, right? Ah, but it'll really pay off in the form of future income. Here are some statistics you should know: A person with a bachelor's degree—which is a four-year college degree—will earn, on average, nearly twice as much as someone with only a high school education. Over a lifetime, in the U.S., that would be $2.1 million, compared to $1.2 million. So you can see why this is my first tip. E4 Number two: Be careful with credit cards. Did you know that in the U.S., the average person's credit card debt is $8,000? That's 8,000. Wow! It can take years to pay that off. So, I'm saying this: Credit is OK if you're careful. It sounds so good, I know, to purchase that new computer or a new pair of jeans now, and pay later. But you have to think about the interest. Say you buy a $1,000-computer, and your annual interest rate is 22 percent. If you don't pay off that charge within one year, up to $220 in interest alone could be added to your bill. And the computer's still not paid for. E5 OK. Next . . . Number three: Have you ever had an emergency and needed money, like for a car repair? We all experience unexpected events, don't we? So, our third strategy for financial success is to prepare for emergencies. How? It's not always easy to save money when we have bills. But here's one idea: Establish a special "emergency" account and regularly deposit a certain amount. Before you spend any of your next paycheck, do this first. Then pay your bills, go out to eat, see a movie—whatever. You'll be pleased at how well this works—and how good you feel knowing you have money to cover your next emergency. E6 Our fourth strategy is this: Invest some of your money. Does this thought make you nervous? It shouldn't—it's not difficult. And by investing, you can really see your money grow. You can start very small. If you're a person who doesn't like taking risks, that's OK. You can put some money in a low-risk fund. If you want help, you can hire a professional to invest for you, someone who's been trained to do this. And, there are books and websites to help you understand how to invest, as well. If you can grow your assets by 5 or 10 percent every year, you'll start to see your money financing your future goals. E7 This brings me to our fifth and final strategy: Save for retirement. I can see some of you are smiling—I know retirement seems far, far away. But by starting early, with your first job, you can set aside small amounts. And that will grow so you can retire in comfort when the time comes. Don't neglect this important step along the road to financial freedom. E8 To wrap up, we all know that happiness does not depend upon money. But financial security can provide a feeling of personal security—and allow you to live the life you want. We can look forward to a secure financial future by using these five strategies: One: Get a college degree. Two: Be careful with credit cards. Three: Prepare for emergencies. Four: Invest. And five: Save for retirement. OK? That's all for today.

Coaching Tips

[1] **Listening: Recognizing imperatives** What is the speaker's advice here? That you get a college degree. Right. Did you hear an imperative verb used with this first tip? What was it? If you said *Get*, you're right! The speaker's way of speaking is a stronger way of saying, "I think you should get . . . " When people give orders or advice, they might use imperatives. Recognizing imperatives in this lecture will help you identify when the speaker is giving her next tip.

[2] Note-taking: Noting numbers When a speaker gives exact numbers, it's a good idea to write these in your notes. So far, you've heard several different numbers and statistics. Here's how you may have noted them: [see video for note-taking example].

[3] Critical Thinking: Predicting Have you experienced an unexpected event, and needed money for it? The speaker is asking this for a reason—she's readying you for her next tip. What do you think it will be? It might be helpful to think about the kinds of tips she's already given. Write your prediction down. Then listen on to see if you are right.

[4] Listening: Guessing "See your money grow." Is this expression new to you? Try to guess what it means. Here are some hints: Think about the lecture topic. Then think about what the speaker has advised so far. In general, what is she suggesting you do with your money? If a lecturer uses an expression that you don't understand, mark it in your notes and ask a classmate or the speaker for clarification after class. Or, research it on your own—and "grow" your vocabulary!

Talk about the Topic *page 80*

Michael: So, after hearing that lecture, how financially secure would you say *you* are?

Hannah: You mean, based on the different strategies the lecturer gave?

Michael: Yeah.

Hannah: Well, with the first two, I think I'm doing OK—I've already started on my college degree. And I only have one credit card, which I pay off every month.

Michael: Good for you. What about the other tips she mentioned? Like saving for emergencies, retirement. . . . Wasn't there another one?

Hannah: Yeah, investing. I think that one is the easiest for me. My parents both work in the financial industry.

Michael: You mean, for investment companies?

Hannah: Exactly.

Michael: No way. That's lucky for you, I guess.

Hannah: Yes and no. I mean, growing up with "money money money" as the daily topic of conversation. Well, let's just say that it kind of made me want to do something different with my life.

Michael: I can understand that. But wait, I'm a little confused—why are you studying economics, then?

Hannah: Well, I want to do some kind of environmental work, like for an NGO.

Michael: N-G-O?

Hannah: A non-governmental organization. You know, like Earthscan or Amazon Watch.

Michael: Oh, OK.

Hannah: Yeah, and so, I think there's this connection between economics and the world's environmental problems.

Michael: Very cool. Well, I'm just trying to understand my own personal economics, starting by paying off my credit cards bills. Do you have any advice for me there?

Hannah: Uh, no not really, I'm all out of ideas.

Michael: Oh no!

Take the Unit Test

1. What does the speaker believe about the five strategies?
2. What is the first tip?
3. How does completing a college degree help financially?
4. Who will earn more money, according to statistics?
5. What statistic does the speaker give about Americans and credit card debt?
6. What is the speaker's point about interest?
7. What is the connection between emergencies and money?
8. How can you learn more about investing?
9. What probably makes the students smile when the speaker says, "Save for retirement."
10. Which financial strategy does the speaker *not* talk about?

Extend the Topic *page 90*

Note that this activity appears at the end of Unit 5b.

Bart: Hello, everyone, and welcome to "I Know an Idiom When I Hear One!" I'm your host, Bart Renfield. Our contestants today are playing for a grand prize of $25,000. Let's welcome Raymond Sample and Lucinda Wordsmart. Let's get started. Here's how our idiom game works. Our theme tonight is money, so all of our idioms are about money. The first person to correctly use the idiom in a sentence gets 100 points. Ready?

Raymond: I'm ready!

Lucinda: Ready, Bart!

Bart: Here's the first idiom: "to burn a hole in one's pocket."

Bart: Raymond!

Raymond: Yes! My paycheck's burning a hole in my pocket! It means I can't wait to spend my money!

Bart: Way to go, Ray! You have 100 points. Next idiom: "to be back on one's feet."

Bart: Lucinda, this one's yours!

Lucinda: Last year I had a lot of financial problems. But now I'm back on my feet!

Bart: Which means . . . ?

Lucinda: Uh . . . I don't have financial problems anymore!

Bart: One hundred points for Lucinda! Great job, Lucinda! Next: "to break the bank" . . .

Build Your Vocabulary *page 75*

B. 1. established 2. invest 3. requires 4. statistics 5. interest 6. debt 7. earn 8. annual 9. deposit 10. credit cards **C. Interact with Vocabulary!** 1. gave us tips about 2. some of your hopes and dreams 3. providing well for your family 4. the first step toward 5. lots of time and money 6. earns more money than 7. to be careful with 8. go into debt 9. prepare for emergencies by 10. pleased at how well this

Focus Your Attention *page 77*

A. Finish your studies, **Save** some money for emergencies, **Don't use** credit cards if you don't have to **B.** 1) your studies 2) Save some money for emergencies 3) Don't use credit cards if you don't have to

Listen for Main Ideas *page 78*

B. Topic: Tips for Financial Success 2. Be careful w/ credit cards 3. Prepare for emergencies 4. Invest some money 5. Save for retirement

Listen for Details *pages 78–79*

B. 1. c 2. a 3. c 4. a 5. b 6. a 7. c

Talk about the Topic *page 80*

A. 1. Hannah 2. Hannah 3. Hannah **B.** 1. Asking for opinions or ideas 2. Asking for clarification or confirmation 3. Asking for clarification or confirmation 4. Asking for clarification or confirmation

Review Your Notes *page 81*

a. big **investment** II. Credit cards: be **careful!** a. debt = **$8,000** III. Prepare for **emergencies** a. establish **emergency** account b. regularly **deposit $** IV. **Invest** money b. hire a **professional** c. **books** and **websites** help you understand V. Save for **retirement** b. set aside **small amounts**

Take the Unit Test

1. a 2. b 3. c 4. b 5. a 6. a 7. b 8. b 9. a 10. b

Extend the Topic *page 90*

Note that this activity appears at the end of Unit 5b. **A.** 1. Money idioms; $25,000; by correctly using money idiom in a sentence

 5a TEST ECONOMICS: Five Tips for Your Financial Future

Listen to each question. Circle the letter of the correct answer.

1. a. that they will help create a strong financial future
   b. that they will stop emergencies
   c. that they are very difficult to do

2. a. Get a job.
   b. Complete a college degree.
   c. Invest your savings.

3. a. It's inexpensive.
   b. It can take a lot of time.
   c. It will help you earn more money later.

4. a. a person who graduated from high school only
   b. a person who has a four-year degree
   c. a person who gets a job after high school

5. a. The average American has about $8,000 in credit card debt.
   b. It takes most Americans eight years to pay off credit cards.
   c. On average, Americans have eight credit cards.

6. a. When you buy something with a credit card, you should think about the interest.
   b. You can buy a computer for $220.
   c. Interest on a new pair of jeans is about 22 percent.

7. a. If you have money, you don't have emergencies.
   b. If you have an emergency, you'll probably need money.
   c. Emergencies are impossible to save for.

8. a. by not taking risks
   b. by hiring an investment professional
   c. by being nervous

9. a. They think they're too young to think about retirement.
   b. They know the speaker is about to retire.
   c. They think it's a joke.

10. a. saving for retirement
    b. using credit cards to save money
    c. investing money

TEACHING TIPS

UNIT OVERVIEW

In this unit, students will learn about Muhammad Yunus's use of microcredit as an agent of economic development. The lecture focuses on the development of the Village Bank, its differences from traditional lending institutions, and its impact on the lives of the poor.

Connect to the Topic *page 82*   *~10 minutes*

Students complete a survey exploring their attitudes toward the poor. Survey questions concern perceived reasons and possible remedies for poverty.

Build Your Vocabulary *pages 83–84*   *~15 minutes*

Students study these words and phrases related to economics and microcredit:

borrow (money)	get credit	(got a) loan
change the	impact	makes loans
lives (of)	impact on	(made a) profit
do business	individual	purchase
earn money	labored	social pressure
exclude	lends	traditional

For the Interact with Vocabulary! activity, you may want to encourage students to first notice the boldfaced words and explain that they form collocations when paired with the correct word.

Focus Your Attention *page 85*   *~10 minutes*

Students hear an excerpt demonstrating how speakers say numbers, and practice note-taking with these symbols:

K	thousand	¢	cent	♀	female/women
M	million	£	pound	♂	male/men
B	billion	~	approx/about	△	change
%	percentage	=	equals	/	per/each/or

Listen to the Lecture *pages 86–87*   *~30 minutes*

Students consider a situation involving poverty (Before You Listen) before listening to the unit lecture on microcredit. Students then identify and order main ideas (Listen for Main Ideas). Next they complete a checklist identifying the practices of three credit sources (Listen for Details).

Lecture video time: 6 min. 57 sec.   *Number of episodes: 11*

Talk about the Topic   *page 88*   *~20 minutes*

Two students—Molly and May—discuss the lecture. Part A focuses on matching these students with comments or ideas from the discussion. In Part B, students work on these discussion strategies:

- Expressing an opinion: "When you think about it, pretty much everyone has *something* to give."
- Disagreeing: "I wouldn't say it quite like that—that the problem is just 'out there.'"
- Offering a fact or example: "I babysit for free one night a week for my neighbor."

For Part C, students are encouraged to use the discussion strategies they've learned. They may use phrases from the student discussion or come up with their own. Keep in mind that some students may not have prior experience or familiarity with the concept of volunteerism, while others may have had extensive experience as volunteers.
Student discussion video time: 1 min. 43 sec.

Review Your Notes   *page 89*   *~15 minutes*

Students focus on reconstructing their notes, paying attention to main ideas, contrasting details, and examples.

BONUS ACTIVITY

You can supplement this activity with an exploration of microcredit development in other countries. Working in small groups, students can gather information about successful microcredit programs and present to the class.

Take the Unit Test   *Teacher's Pack page 61*   *~15 minutes*

You may want to play the lecture again just before giving the test. Students answer standard test questions about the content of the lecture. Specifically, the test covers the following: definition of microcredit, characteristics of traditional banks, characteristics of the Village Bank, and impact of the Village Bank on the lives of the poor.

Extend the Topic   *page 91*   *~30 minutes,*

- Listening and Discussion: Students listen to and discuss a clip about how an organization started by two volunteers has impacted the lives of poor, urban children.
- Project/Presentation: Students interview three volunteers and present their findings to the class.

Focus Your Attention:
Try It Out! *page 85*

Speaker: Every year, more and more people don't make enough money to feed their families. From 1983 to 1993, about 1.1 billion people became poorer. Today, 2.9 billion people live on less than two dollars a day. And did you know that 70 percent of those people are women? If we do not make some changes, by 2030 we will have 4.9 billion or more people living on only two dollars per day.

Listen for Main Ideas and Listen
for Details *pages 86–87*

Economics lecturer: E1 Today I'd like to talk about world economics. In particular, I want to look at one idea that's improving the lives of many poor people. This idea is called the "Village Bank." It was started by a man named Muhammad Yunus, an economics professor in Bangladesh. Let's talk first about why Professor Yunus started the bank. Then we'll look at how the bank has changed people's lives. **E2** In 1974, a famine killed more than 1.5 million people in Bangladesh. Professor Yunus saw thousands of poor and sick people coming into his city, looking for work and food. He knew that somehow, economics could reduce their suffering. **E3** To study this idea further, he went to a Bengali village to learn more about the lives of the poor. There, he talked with many people. For example, he met Sugai Begum, a single mother who bought food for her three children by making bamboo stools—these are like, small chairs. **E4** Each day Sugai got money from money lenders, called "middlemen." She'd take five taka (or about twenty-two cents U.S.) and use that money to buy bamboo, which—interestingly—was sold by these same middlemen who'd loaned her the money. Hmmm . . . Well, then she'd labor all day making bamboo stools. And at the end of the day, she'd sell them for a total of five taka and fifty paisa—or about twenty-four cents total. So, after working all day, she'd earned a total of two cents! And guess who purchased the stools? Right—those same middlemen. **E5** Now, her bamboo stools were worth much more on the free market. But the middlemen were the only people who'd lend her money. They controlled the market. So, as you can see, there was an economic problem here. **E6** Well, Sugai wasn't alone. Professor Yunus talked to other villagers and learned that many were just like her, in this same strange business relationship with the middlemen. So Professor Yunus loaned each of these people the money they needed—about sixty-two U.S. cents per person. This freed them from the middlemen—and let them buy and sell on the open market. And guess what? All of them were able to pay Professor Yunus back. **E7** So, Professor Yunus had found a new way to fight poverty—with microcredit: m-i-c-r-o. Microcredit. That is, making small loans to poor people so they can grow their businesses, and earn more money. Well, then, Professor Yunus tried to take this discovery to traditional international banks. But they weren't interested in lending money to the poor. They didn't believe that poor people could earn the money they'd need to repay their loans. **E8** So Professor Yunus and a few others decided to start a bank that would be very different from traditional banks—in three important ways. First, unlike traditional banks that require people to already have some money in order to get a loan, the Village Bank gives loans to the poorest people. This means giving loans to mostly women because about 97 percent of the world's poor are women. Second, traditionally, banks give loans to individuals or companies. But the Village Bank works with small groups, usually five to ten people. The group members decide who's the poorest, and those people get their loans first. Everyone else receives their loans only after the neediest members have repaid theirs. So members feel support, but also social pressure to work hard and repay their loans. **E9** The third way the Village Bank differs from traditional banks is location. Most banks are in cities, right? And who does that exclude? Yup, villagers. So, the Village Bank has set up more than 2,000 branches throughout villages in Bangladesh. And each branch has what are called "bicycle managers." Why? Because they go by bicycle to borrowers' houses where they discuss how business is going and give advice. **E10** Now, do these small loans really have an impact on people's lives? Well, I think the story of Riziya Begum will answer that. For years, Riziya lived with her family in Bangladesh in great poverty, some days having nothing to eat. Then one day she went to the Village Bank and got a $30 loan. With the loan, she bought a cow. In turn, she began selling things like milk and butter. She then used that money to buy more cows. After a while, she'd saved enough money to buy land. Then, she sold the land, and used those profits to send her son to Saudi Arabia to work. From the money he sent home to her, she bought more land and sent her daughter to school—the first girl in the family to get an education. **E11** So, on a $30-loan, Riziya Begum moved from poor to middle-class. It's quite a success story, huh? And this story is typical among Village Bank borrowers. About 64 percent of them have crossed over the poverty line. So, you tell me, can a little loan make a big difference?

Coaching Tips

[1] Note-taking: Using abbreviations The speaker says that in 1974, 1.5 million people in Bangladesh died. One way to write *1.5 million* is *1,500,000*. But a long number like this takes time to write, and uses a lot of space in your notes. A faster way to write this number is to use an abbreviation. Do you remember the abbreviation for *million*? If you said *M*, you're right! You can write this number very quickly if you use this abbreviation. Your notes might look like this: [see video for note-taking example]. Try to listen for other numbers in this lecture and see if you can think of ways to write them quickly using abbreviations.

[2] Note-taking and Listening: Order The speaker tells about a day in the life of Sugai Begum. She tells each important event in the order that it happens by using signal words and phrases such as *each day, then, at the end of the day,* and *after working all day.* By listening for these signal words, you can understand the order in which each event in the story happens. To show the order of these events in your notes, you can use an arrow symbol. Your notes might look like this: [see video for note-taking example].

[3] Critical Thinking: Using your imagination What does the speaker mean here by "strange business relationship"? From what you know about business and economics, what is strange, or wrong, about the situation that Sugai was in? Imagine yourself in Sugai's situation, or in a similar situation. What about it would be difficult? How would you fix it?

[4] Critical Thinking: Identifying point of view After she tells the story of Riziya Begum, the speaker says, "It's quite a success story, huh?" She then adds, "So you tell me, can a little loan make a big difference?" Does the speaker want answers to these questions? Probably not. In this case, she's actually expressing an opinion—and believes you'll agree. Speakers may also end statements with words like "right?" or "correct?" By using these kinds of questions, speakers show their point of view. And knowing a speaker's point of view can help you decide how to process the information they give.

Talk about the Topic *page 88*

Molly: Wow, that lecture gave me a lot of hope about helping people in poverty, you know?

May: Oh, I know exactly what you're saying. Those examples made me feel so good. But I still think we need to remember that the Village Bank is just one project. And there's still a lot of poverty out there.

Molly: True. But I wouldn't quite say it like that—that it's just "out there." I mean, it's everywhere. Even in developed countries, there are poor people.

May: I know. I mean, poverty doesn't have a nationality. It just seems that sometimes some people get themselves in bad situations. And, they need help.

Molly: Exactly. And a little help can make a big difference, just like we saw in the lecture.

May: Uh-huh. What about you yourself? Do you do anything to help fight poverty?

Molly: Well, I don't know if it's helping to fight poverty. But I babysit for free one night a week for my neighbor. She has kind of a hard time financially. And she works at a hospital, so the nights that I babysit, she might work late, or go get groceries, or whatever. It just gives her a little extra time.

May: Yeah, that's cool.

Molly: What about you?

May: Yeah, I started volunteering at an after-school program, helping kids with math.

Molly: It's volunteer work?

May: Yeah, I don't get paid, but I really enjoy teaching them—and they appreciate it.

Molly: That's great. In my opinion, giving someone a skill is just as good as giving or loaning them money.

May: For sure. And, I mean, if you think about it, pretty much everyone has *something* to give.

Molly: You said it. Hey, maybe you can give me some review questions about the lecture.

May: Oh yeah, no problem. OK, how was the Village Bank started?

Molly: Professor Yunus in Bangladesh decided he wanted to fight poverty . . .

Take the Unit Test

1. What is the main idea of the lecture?
2. Why did Professor Yunus start to think about ways to help poor people?
3. How much money did Sugai Begum earn after working all day?
4. How were Bengali villagers able to repay Dr. Yunus? Choose *two* answers.
5. What does "microcredit" mean?
6. Why don't traditional banks loan money to the poor?
7. Who does the Village Bank mostly work with? Choose *two* answers.
8. What do bicycle managers do?
9. What does the story of the Riziya Begum and her $30-loan show?
10. How does the speaker feel about the Village Bank?

Extend the Topic *page 91*

Documentarian: Today Adam and Emma Parker received the Carson City Excellence Award for their service to this city's children. Twenty years ago, the Parkers started The Hang-Out as a place for children to come after school to play, talk, and get help doing their schoolwork. The Parkers have helped hundreds of children feel safe, supported, and loved.

Girl: I almost live at The Hang-Out, you know? I mean, this feels like home. The Parkers are cool people. They make us feel important.

Boy: Yeah. We're all good friends here. And, like with me, now I enjoy going to school. I think about college . . .

Girl: Me, too. I'm definitely going to college.

Boy: Yeah. Me, I'm thinking about studying engineering.

Girl: I think I want to do something with politics, maybe. Like Tasha. She's a community organizer.

Documentarian: Tasha is just one of many volunteers who work with the kids at The Hang-Out. As a kid, Tasha used to come to The Hang-Out herself, so she knows what these kids need . . .

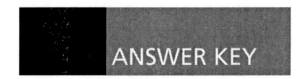

ANSWER KEY

Build Your Vocabulary *page 83*

B. 1. individual 2. borrow 3. loan 4. traditional
5. exclude 6. purchase 7. lend 8. impact
9. labored 10. profit; **C. Interact with Vocabulary!**
1. makes, X 2. earn, X 3. getting, X 4. change, the 5. sold, a 6. a, do 7. social, your 8. X, on

Focus Your Attention *page 85*

A. a **B.** 2.9 B, <$2, ♀; 2030: 4.9, $2

Listen for Main Ideas *page 86*

B. Not discussed: The Village Bank has more money than a traditional bank. Traditional banks are in old buildings; 2, 3, 5, 4, 1

Listen for Details *page 87*

B. A money lender: 1, 2, 4, 5, 6; A traditional bank: 7; The Village Bank: 1, 3, 4, 8, 9, 10

Talk about the Topic *page 88*

A. 1. Molly, May 2. Molly, May 3. Molly, May
B. 1. Disagreeing 2. Offering a fact or example
3. Offering a fact or example (Note: May actually says, "I started . . .") 4. Expressing an opinion (Note: May actually says, "*If* you think . . ." not "When.")

Review Your Notes *page 89*

Notes on **Microcredit and the Village Bank**
1) a. 1974, 1.5M b. poverty, middlemen c. 62¢
d. loans, middlemen, sell on open e. small loans, poor people 2) Traditional Banks a. poor people, $
b. small groups, companies c. villages, cities
3) b. the poverty line

Take the Unit Test

1. b 2. c 3. a 4. a and b 5. c 6. c 7. a and c
8. b 9. a 10. b

UNIT 5b TEST ECONOMICS: Microcredit: Changing Lives

Listen to each question. Circle the letter of the correct answer.

1. a. how people become poor
   b. how microcredit can help poor people
   c. how banks operate

2. a. He wanted to start a bank.
   b. He liked to study economics.
   c. He saw many poor people looking for work and food.

3. a. 2 cents
   b. 22 cents
   c. Nothing. She owed the middlemen.

4. a. by buying and selling on the open market
   b. by investing in their businesses
   c. by borrowing from the middlemen

5. a. making small loans to middlemen
   b. borrowing money from banks
   c. making small loans to poor people

6. a. because the poor can't earn money to pay back the money
   b. because the banks are not interested in making money
   c. because the banks don't believe the poor can repay the loans

7. a. small groups
   b. bicycle shop owners
   c. women

8. a. collect payments
   b. give financial advice
   c. deliver money

9. a. how small loans can change people's lives
   b. what people can buy with their loans
   c. how the Village Bank is like traditional banks

10. a. She's not sure it works.
    b. She thinks it's a success.
    c. She doesn't say.

Credits

Unit 1: *Collapse: How Societies Choose to Fail or Succeed* by J. Diamond; "Cracking the Khipu code," *Science 300*; "New Grange: A passage to the afterworld" and "Newgrange megalithic passage tomb" at knowth.com; "Petroglyphs" at netaxs.com; "Apocolypse" by G. Phillips at grahamphillips.net; *1,000 Places to See Before You Die* by P. Schultz; *The Collapse of Complex Societies* by J. A. Tainter; "Archaeoastronomy at Stonehenge" by L. C. E. Witcombe at witcombe.sbc.edu **Unit 2:** *Third Culture Kids* by David C. Pollock and Ruth E. Van Reken; U.S. Department of State at state.gov; "Third Culture Kids: Returning to Their Passport Country" by Julie K. Kidd and Linda L. Lankenau, *Syllabus*; "Third Culture Kids: Focus of Major Study" by Ruth Hill Useem at iss.edu **Unit 3:** "Compulsive eating: Trigger foods and opioids" at nutramed.com; "Food addiction—are you a food addict?" at allaboutlifechallenges.org; "The traffic light diet" by J. Kellow at weightlossresources.co.uk; "Western influences disrupt Mediterranean diet" by J. Shapiro, *Global Health, NPR Weekend Edition*; "Better information, better health" at webmd.com; "The Mediterranean diet: Can it reduce your risk for heart disease?" at womensheartfoundation.org **Unit 4:** "Culture-Based Negotiation Styles" and "Communication Tools for Understanding Cultural Differences" by Michelle LeBaron at beyondintractability.org; *The Art of Crossing Cultures* by Craig Storti; *Managing Cultural Differences* by Robert T. Moran, Philip R. Harris, and Sarah V. Moran; *Figuring Foreigners Out* by Craig Storti; "Effective Multicultural International Business Meetings" by Neil Payne at culturosity.com and kwintessential.co.uk; "Managing Cross-Cultural Differences in International Projects" by Lionel Laroche at itapintl.com; "Key Team Personalities" by Jeff Palfini at bnet.com; *Developing the Global Organization* by Robert T. Moran, Philip R. Harris, and William G. Stripp; "We Can't Go On Meeting Like This" at lanzen.co.uk **Unit 5:** *The Nine Steps to Financial Freedom* by S. Orman; "10 financial tips for young people" at bankrate.com; "Grameen Bank: Taking Capitalism to the Poor" by Evaristus Mainsuh, Schuyler R. Heuer, Aprajita Kaira, and Qiulin Zhang at gsb.columbia.edu; "Saving the World One Cup of Yogurt at a Time" by Sheridan Prasso, *Fortune Magazine*; "What is Microcredit?" and "Grameen Microcredit and How to End Poverty from the Roots Up" by Paul Sinclair at grameen-info.org